Praise for *Worship Together in*]
as in Heaven

"Worship must come from the heart to be authentic. Our expressions of authentic worship are seeded in our respective cultures. Davis and Lerner provide steps to help us grow in our personal development to lead a multicultural worship service that is an authentic reflection of the various cultures in your congregation."

—Art Lucero, Pastor, Sunrise Church High Desert, Victorville, CA

"Through the church God gathers the world to himself—embracing but transcending the rich diversity of nationalities, ethnicities, and cultures. As someone who is actively involved with the heart of this book in both academic and local church contexts, I enthusiastically commend its impassioned call to study, implement, and lead multicultural worship of the one true God that reflects the beautiful and broad ethnic mosaic of his global church. Josh Davis and Nikki Lerner have created an essential and practical guide that every worship leader, pastor, and church leader needs to read, learn, digest, and practice."

—James R. Hart, President, Robert E. Webber Institute for Worship Studies, Orange Park, FL

"More than a unique description of how to navigate worship leading in a culturally diverse church, Lerner and Davis's superb book is a practical resource for connection and community building in any environment. In fact I will be using some of their suggestions to relate to my fairly nondiverse congregation this very weekend."

—Lance Winkler, Director of Contemporary Worship, The United Methodist Church of the Resurrection, Leawood, KS

"What a delightful and challenging read! This innovative book offers a wealth of good theology, encouraging case studies, life-tested models, and strategies for developing multicultural worship in all kinds of communities. We've been waiting for this book for a long time, and I can hardly wait to study it with my own worship team! Covering important topics like the dangers of monocultural worship, using what's in your hand, and what to do when the process is discouraging, this book will be required reading for the ethnodoxology courses I teach!"

—Robin P. Harris, President, International Council of Ethnodoxologists; Director, Center for Excellence in World Arts, Dallas, TX

"*Multicultural* is more than a buzzword; it's God's desire for the church. The challenge is to be more than "multicultural" in name only by truly reflecting it through worship. Davis and Lerner's practical approach gives guidance in the "how-to" of incorporating diversity through corporate worship."
—Rosario Picardo, Executive Pastor of New Church Development, Ginghamsburg Church, Tipp City, OH

"Lerner and Davis have vast experience in multicultural ministry that is practical, transferable, artistic, and spiritually discerned. They and their readers will bless the world with the art and grace of inclusion."
—David A. Anderson, Senior Pastor of Bridgeway Community Church, Baltimore, MD

"Nikki and Josh are experienced, respected, and credible voices delivering much needed, specialized, instruction for the growing number of churches seeking to reflect God's love for all people, not just one kind of people, through worship arts. Toward that end, their book will help you identify the questions, take intentional steps, and promote a spirit of inclusion through worship arts and in the process help you build a healthy multiethnic church for the sake of the gospel in an increasingly diverse society."
—Mark DeYmaz, Lead Pastor, Mosaic Church of Central Arkansas; author of *Leading a Healthy Multi-Ethnic Church*

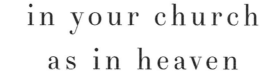

Worship Together

in your church
as in heaven

Josh Davis/Nikki Lerner

Abingdon Press

Nashville

WORSHIP TOGETHER IN YOUR CHURCH AS IN HEAVEN

This book is printed on acid-free paper.

Library of Congress Cataloging-in-Publication Data has been requested.

ISBN: 978-1-4267-8806-2

15 16 17 18 19 20 21 22 23 24—10 9 8 7 6 5 4 3 2 1
MANUFACTURED IN THE UNITED STATES OF AMERICA

This work is dedicated to all of you who are embracing the vision and the mission of intentional multicultural ministry. To all of you who are leading and serving God's people and have a longing to see worship on earth as it is in heaven—multicultural and glorious—we pass on what we've learned so far on this journey. To all of you who are doing the hard work of becoming bridge-builders for God's diverse people and who might be wondering if you are crazy for pursuing this amazing calling, this work is for you. Lean in. Lead well. Persevere, and keep loving God's people. It is worth it!

They took up a new song, saying,
"You are worthy to take the scroll and open its seals,
because you were slain,
and by your blood you purchased for God
persons from every tribe, language, people, and nation."

—Revelation 5:9

새 노래를 노래하여 가로되 책을 가지시고 그 인봉을 떼기에 합당하시도
다 일찍 죽임을 당하사 각 족속과 방언과 백성과 나라 가운데서 사람들을
피로 사서 하나님께 드리시고

—요한계시록 5:9

If you want to go fast, go alone. If you want to go far, go together.

—African proverb

إذا اردت الذهاب سريعا اذهب لوحدك، إذا اردت الذهاب بعيدا فلنذهب معاً.

—مثل افريقي

Worship at its best is a social experience with people of all levels of life
coming together to realize their oneness and unity under God.

—Martin Luther King Jr., *The Words of Martin Luther King Jr.*

La adoración en su mejor momento es una experiencia social con personas
de todos los niveles de la vida reunidos para darse cuenta de su unidad
bajo Dios.

—Martin Luther King Jr., *The Words of Martin Luther King Jr.*

Contents

Section III: Hamstrings, *American Idol*, and Didgeridoos [Leading change for the greater good]

Section IV: Grab Your Wrench! [The nuts and bolts of multicultural worship leading]

Chapter 14: Worship in Different Languages

Don't underestimate the power of language. Here's a step-by-step process for introducing multiple languages in worship.

Section V: On Earth as It Is in Heaven
[It's not always easy. But, it's always worth it!]

Chapter 15: Models of Multicultural Worship

Here are four basic models of multiethnic worship and the benefits and challenges for each. Which one might be helpful for you?

Chapter 16: Surviving the Hard Times

Here are some practical tips for when things get rough, and they will.

Chapter 17: Stories of Encouragement

We are each surrounded by such a great cloud of witnesses. Multicultural worship is happening successfully all around this globe. Take a look!

Section I

Worship Together

[Because we want to . . . because he said so]

Chapter 1
Who Are We?

*Stories are important. Where people come from is important. History
affects the present and the future. Get to know us.*

Josh's Story

I grew up in (was born into really!) a church that loved music and the
nations. It has taken me until today to fully realize it because they were so
. . . well . . . reserved. I can remember discussions during Sunday lunch about
someone who started the clapping after a special music number at church.
Clapping was not forbidden, but it certainly was not welcomed either. I can
remember the few people whom I ever saw raise their hands in worship. None
of them had grown up in our church. They were outsiders, transplants. And I
remember the very few people who sang loud enough to be heard by someone
sitting two pews in front of them. My mom was one of those high-volume
singers. It used to embarrass me. Now, I am quite proud. It's funny how perspectives change.

I grew up in an all-White, traditional church. We sang hymns. Lots of
them. All the time. Except, I can remember once when "Jews for Jesus" came
and sang some Messianic music. It was so different. So other. So captivating.
I went around for weeks after singing "Jehovah-Jireh, my Provider, His grace
is sufficient for me, for me, for me."[1] And then, I can remember when we
started a contemporary service at 8:00 a.m., and some girls sang a song out of
a chorus book and were accompanied only by the piano. And I can remember
the controversy those choruses caused.

---

1. Merla Watson, "Jehovah-Jireh," MCA Music Publ., A.D.O. Universal Studio, 1974.

I grew up in a very missions-minded church. Which means we had a missionary's name in the bulletin every week for us to pray for. And we had a map on the wall in the foyer with a bunch of people's pictures attached to it. And we had missions conferences. Every year. And I loved them! I loved getting to dress up in a traditional costume and carry a flag from another country. I loved getting the chance to have missionaries in our home for lunch or dinner. I loved hearing their stories and learning about other cultures. I loved going to their seminars and seeing slide shows of different people and places. I especially loved it when they let us use their blowguns or we would try to translate words from an unknown language using some principles they taught us. I learned so many good things growing up in my church. I learned to love God's word. I learned how to be a community that knows and cares for one another. I learned about what God was doing in other parts of the world. My church loved the nations, and I am grateful. But, practically speaking, we loved the nations from a distance and with special fervor during one week each year. We never sang the songs of the nations. We rarely, if ever, loved the nations in our midst.

The town I lived in had what was called "Newtown," which was the neighborhood, centered around MLK Jr. Boulevard, where most of the African Americans lived. I lived in an all-White neighborhood, was home-schooled (mostly), and went to an all-White church until I was thirteen years old. At which time, my family moved first to Costa Rica and then to the Dominican Republic to become missionaries. My life radically changed on so many levels. I began to learn Spanish and strangely found that I not only was good at it but also quite enjoyed it. Something in me came alive when I spoke Spanish. My friends would say that I sounded like an entirely different person when I was speaking Spanish. It was in the Dominican Republic that I began to experience worship in a different way. All of the sudden, I was part of a church that was very expressive in their worship. They sang loudly. They clapped their hands. They raised their hands. They prayed prayers out loud and for extended periods of time. And something in me came alive. This was more like how I expressed my worship to God in private. And in my church in the Dominican Republic, I had the freedom to do so in public.

When I came back to the United States, however, I found some interesting things. I have found that I no longer fit in one world or another. I am not entirely at home in the United States. I do not fit completely in the Dominican Republic either. I like to call myself a multicultural mutt. On the outside

I look simple enough. White. American, like the cheese. But can you tell by looking that the American in me is time oriented and values productivity while the Dominican in me is event oriented and values relationship? Can you tell by looking at me that I have a Sudanese friend whose heart is so similar to mine that we call each other twin brothers? Never mind that he is well over six feet tall and his skin is as black as I have ever seen. Can you tell by looking at me that I can sing worship songs in more than eighteen languages off the top of my head and that, on any given day, one of those songs might come out of my mouth and my heart during my own personal time with the Lord? Can you tell that my first choice for worship music is gospel music and my second choice is Hindi? Can you tell by looking at me that I am learning American Sign Language so that I can communicate with my Deaf neighbor? Can you tell that I have been in worship leadership in a Baptist church, a nondenominational church, a United Methodist church, and a Mennonite Charismatic church? Can you tell by looking at me what church I should go to? Or what church I shouldn't go to?

I have two heart languages, English and Spanish. I have also found that more often than not, I have to choose whether I will be American or Latino when I go to church. Will I sing in English or Spanish? It is this tension inside me that in many ways has led me to consider why the body of Christ is so segregated when it comes to worship. It is this tension, combined with the power of the word of God that has led me to found Proskuneo Ministries (www.proskuneo.org). Proskuneo exists to glorify God and promote unity in the body of Christ through multilingual, multicultural worship gatherings, worship resources, and training in order that lives may be transformed and nations come together to worship God. In the last eleven years, I have devoted my life to seeing multicultural worship happen. And I fully expect to live the rest of my life praying for and working toward that glimpse of God's kingdom come on earth as it is in heaven.

Our Friendship

I have a few people in my life who I can remember distinctly the moment I met them. Nikki is the *only* person who I can remember seeing as a stranger in a crowd before I met her. We were both traveling to a conference in New Orleans, and she came from Maryland and had to change planes in Atlanta. It just so happened we were on the same plane from Atlanta to New Orleans.

And I can remember seeing her in the waiting area. She had a presence. (She still does!) She was confident and gracious. My wife says she is regal. I agree. It wasn't until hours later that we saw each other again in the lobby of the conference hotel and realized that we were brother and sister in Christ and both had a passion for multicultural worship. Amazing! I immediately sensed a family bond with Nikki (and we have some ridiculous pictures to prove it!), but I had no idea that I would be so profoundly affected by her and so incredibly blessed by her friendship and partnership in ministry. Now, only a few years later, we have written songs together, cotaught at conferences, led worship together, and ministered together on every coast of the United States and internationally! We have led and taught and loved each other's people. Our families have vacationed together. We have prayed for each other, challenged each other, asked each other difficult questions. And now, we are writing a book together. We love doing life together and worshipping God together.

We are learning what it is to work together. To lean on each other's strengths. To cover for each other's weaknesses. We understand that we are better together than we are apart. There have been many times that she said something I couldn't say, or said it in a way that I could never have said it. And vice versa. We are learning never to underestimate the impact of diverse people working together. We have been told many times that even the visual of me and Nikki leading and following each other is powerful. I have a tremendous amount of respect for Nikki's thoughtful leadership. She is a reflector. She has a gift of connecting with people and setting people at ease in her presence. People are drawn to her. She is courageous in the face of conflict, and when she knows what needs to be done, she does it, unapologetically. She challenges, empowers, and frees the people she leads to become leaders. I have a lot to learn from her. And I am looking forward to what I will learn, even as we coauthor this book.

Nikki's Story

"Jesus who?" That sort of sums up my knowledge of all things God-related until I was thirteen years old. I grew up in a very loving and good family. Church or anything having to do with God was not a part of our history as a family or even something that we valued. We were, however, what a friend of mine would call "Cheasters" (pronounced *Chee-sters*). We would occasionally go to church on Christmas and Easter with my grandmother, Elaine. I think

6

that our family had some sort of belief in a "higher power," but now as I think about it, we may not have even had that. What I do remember is that there actually were times when I would ask to go to church with my grandmother. I think most of that was just to spend time with her, but I remember that I had the desire to go, nonetheless. It wasn't until my freshman year of high school that I was introduced to matters of faith. I was invited to a weekend retreat with an organization called Young Life by my volleyball team captain. Honestly, the only reason I went was that I thought it would be cool to hang out with her. It was at this retreat that I first heard about Jesus and that I could actually have a relationship with him. My response to the gospel went something like this: "Well, that just makes sense." And now, here I am, walking faithfully with Christ. Jesus sought me out and initiated his presence in my life, and now I am forever changed. In fact, that is one of my very own names for God, "the Initiator."

Apparently, I was never "Black enough." Or at least, that's what I was told by some members of my family. Not all of them, mind you. My mother's side of the family had always lived very multicultural lives. I am grateful for that as I write this today. People of many different races always surrounded us, and we always lived in communities that were multicultural. I had friends of different ethnicities, and I dated, romantically, outside of my race throughout the years. For the other members of my family, this multicultural lifestyle posed a particular problem. I remember my stepfather asking me to please initiate more friendships with African American kids. I remember some family members giving me a hard time because my boyfriends were not Black. When I asked them what the big deal was, their response was that they were concerned that I would lose sight of my heritage, my "Blackness." I remember being accused of "talking White" because I did not have a particular accent that could be associated with some African American cultures. I was even told by a family member that teachers in my school only liked me because I had White friends and because I wasn't really a Black person at all. It was tough at times. I believe that I could have had a huge identity crisis had it not been for a few strong women in my family (namely, my mother, her sister, and my grandmother) who taught me that people were the same no matter what their skin color and heritage. Not only that, but also they were to be affirmed, not in spite of, but because of how they were made by God. It is this heritage along with observing the tension between these two worldviews that are an important piece of the tapestry of my life and passion today.

I am married to a wonderful man who is White. Given what you just read, that's a big shocker, right? Contrary to some opinion, I didn't go out looking for a White man, and I didn't marry him because of his money (which he doesn't have) or any reason other than the fact that I am smart and I know a gift from the Lord when I see one. My husband, David, and I had been dating for less than one month when he proposed to me. I know, I know, that sounds crazy, right? But have you ever heard married people say something like "when you know, you know"? Well, I knew. While engaged, we thought that it would be important to decide whose church we would attend. There was only one problem: neither of us particularly cared for the other's place of worship. I was almost positive that he would just love the church that I was attending at the time, and I was so excited to bring him there. What I didn't expect to hear from David was the following question, "Where are all the Black people?" Hmmm. Honestly, that had never occurred to me. You see, since beginning to follow Jesus Christ when I was thirteen years old, most of my church experience, with the exception of a two-year experience at an African American Pentecostal church, had been in mostly Caucasian churches. In fact, growing up, I remember that my family was usually one of two or three Black families in a room wherever we went. My Aunt Fannie (God rest her soul) would always say something like, "We are the only chocolate chips in a room full of vanilla wafers." Ha! So, the fact that I was attending a predominantly Caucasian church never seemed to be an issue. I was quite intrigued that my White, soon-to-be husband felt so uncomfortable in such a uni-cultural environment. We decided to look for a church where we both felt comfortable to worship. Our church-search was not an easy one. Because we are an interracial couple, we get stared at wherever we go. My mother-in-law swears that it is just because we are tall, but I think she's just trying to be nice. It was no different for us while trying to find a church home. You tend to stick out when you walk into churches where you are the only ones who are "different." In fact, some studies have shown that couples like us end up not going to church at all because our families stick out and people don't quite know what to do with us.

In 1999, six months before we were to be married, we walked through the doors of Bridgeway Community Church in Columbia, Maryland (www .bridgewayonline.org). A friend of ours found Bridgeway in the phone book and was so excited to call us and tell us about this church that he found. His sales pitch? "There are seven interracial couples here!" That's what he said.

Well, that was enough for us to go check it out. I will never forget what it felt like to walk into the doors of that church. I remember feeling like we finally fit. No one stared. We saw other couples who were like us and couples who were not like us at all! We saw multiracial people and children everywhere! After finding our seat in the meeting space and just taking in everything that we saw, we knew we were home. We were just praying that the church was biblically sound and that the people weren't crazy; well, they are crazy, but a good kind of crazy. We decided to make Bridgeway Community Church our home. Since that time, we have been on the ride of our lives, and God has given us the desire of our hearts—desires that we didn't even know existed. Who could've guessed that we would be ministered to and encouraged not only in our faith but also in our culture as people? Who could've guessed that I would be leading a worship ministry made up of more than one hundred amazing people? Who could've guessed that I would be writing this book and passing along all of the knowledge that the Lord has given me as I benefited from serving him in a beautiful and vibrant multicultural congregation of more than forty-five hundred people? God knew. And I am grateful. The story continues . . .

Our Story

Josh and I met in August of 2009 at a small, fifteen-person retreat in New Orleans, Louisiana. We get a kick out of telling the story of how we were actually on the same flight headed out to New Orleans. Apparently, Josh saw me in the airport terminal, and I noticed him while boarding the plane. He was on the left side of the plane and looked up from reading his book as I was coming down the aisle. Our eyes actually met, and the first thing I thought to myself was, "I wonder if that guy knows Jesus." He just had that look about him—you know, that look?

Later that day, we found ourselves in the same room with a group of about thirteen other worship pastors and leaders. This special group spent two and a half days together, sharing stories, struggles, successes, and strategies with regard to multicultural worship, and ever since then our hearts have been connected.

After our time together at that retreat, we both knew that the Lord had allowed us to meet each other and become friends for a very special purpose. There is a verse in Ephesians 2:21 in which the Apostle Paul says, "We are carefully joined together in him, becoming a holy temple for the Lord" (NLT). I believe that God has Josh and me together to accomplish the work of the kingdom that we could not do apart from each other. We share the same heart and vision for all of God's people to come together in worshipping our great God. Since 2009, we have led worship together, taught classes on multiethnic ministry, cowritten songs together, stayed in each other's homes, ministered to young emerging leaders, and dreamed big about the future together. We believe that two are better than one because they have a good return for their work (Eccl 4:9-12). We believe that writing this book together models the very principles that lie within it. And we really just like working and creating together.

Why Multicultural Worship?

Multicultural worship is not our idea, but God's. It is firmly rooted in God's heart. And we believe that if worship is not diverse, it is dangerous.

A group of my (Josh's) friends gathered in a home one Friday night for a time of worship. Some of my friends who gathered were Burmese, from a particular ethnic group called the Karen (pronounced *kuh-rén*) people. My other friends were White Americans. They desired to have a night of worship together. They visited with one another, and then after a while, one of the White American men got out a guitar and started playing some worship songs. First, they found several songs they all had in common, that the White Americans could sing in English while the Burmese could sing in Karen. After that, the Burmese taught a song or two in Karen to the White Americans. Then, the White Americans taught a song or two in English to the Karen. It was a lovely time. After about forty minutes of singing, however, one of the Burmese men asked a question that startled the White Americans. "When are we going to worship?" he asked. The White Americans thought they already were worshipping. But, clearly, for the Karen, this sharing with one another and singing songs of praise in different languages didn't seem like worship. One group thought they were already worshipping, while the other was waiting to get started.

Because people have such different perspectives on what worship is, and such different ways of expressing worship to God, it is sometimes hard to even know where to begin. Multicultural worship and unity can be incredibly uncomfortable, complicated, difficult, and time consuming. It can require lots of hard work. People have strong opinions about drums and pipe organs, order and flexibility, volume levels and tempos, and the length of songs and sermons. So why bother? Why not settle for worship services suited to your individual tastes and preferences? Many do. But worship has always been and will always be bigger than us, our preferences, our grooves, our desires, our music, our ways. It is more than hands folded or hands raised, fast or slow, loud or soft, active or still.

Many times as we approach the subject of worship, we are asking the wrong questions. What kind of music do we like? What are the felt needs of the congregation? Who is our target audience? In what ways can we best worship God? But, what if, instead, we were to ask the question: what does *God* desire? Ephesians 5:10 exhorts us to "try to discern what is pleasing to the Lord" (ESV). Instead of focusing on what is pleasing to us, let's find out what pleases God. As we look throughout the Scriptures, we see some very important principles.

Many times as we approach the subject of worship, we are asking the wrong questions. What kind of music do we like? What are the felt needs of the congregation? Who is our target audience? In what ways can we best worship God? But, what if, instead, we were to ask the question: what does *God* desire?

God Created the Nations

Acts 17:26 states this clearly. "From one person God created every human nation to live on the whole earth, having determined their appointed times and the boundaries of their lands." From one man, Adam, God made every nation of mankind. Before we go too far, we need to make sure we understand the concept of this word *nation*. In the Greek, this is the word *ethnos,* which is most often translated "nation" in English. We have to be careful, however, not to think of this word as meaning a political or geographic grouping of people. We should think of it more like it is used in the term *Cherokee nation*, which means something like a people with a unifying ethnic identity. *Nations*, according to Scripture, may not have a geopolitical organization or boundary, but they are definitely unified by culture or language. For example, I (Josh) teach piano to some Kurdish students each week. The Kurds are very much an ethnos, but they have no one country that is home for them. Most of them are spread throughout a geographical region that spans the geopolitical boundaries of several nations. Obviously, it is from this word *ethnos* that we get our English terms *ethnic* and *ethnicity*. The biblical premise of this book is that God desires the ethnos to worship him together. In this book, we will deal with issues of race and culture as they relate to different ethnos or ethnic groups, as this is the biblical concept and wording.

Nations, according to Scripture, may not have a geopolitical organization or boundary, but they are definitely unified by culture or language.

From one person, Adam, God made every ethnic group. I can remember processing this reality as a kid. I would sit in the mall and watch different kinds of people walk past me, and I would think, if the Bible is true, then we are all related to one another. If we go back far enough, we will find a common relative. We may have to go all the way back to Noah, but somehow, we are all related. This should have a staggering impact on the way we view the world. This means that Hitler was murdering his relatives. It means that the Shiites and the Sunnis are in the midst of a family feud.

God himself created the diversity of people groups. We see in Genesis 11:1-9 that, because the people were not fulfilling God's desire and commandment for them to spread out and live throughout all the earth, God confused them at the tower of Babel by creating diverse languages. This act was not only a continuation of God's creative process but also a way of fulfilling his purpose to spread out people over all the earth.

Even when God was blessing Abraham, God was blessing the nations. His heart has always been for the nations he has created. It is easy to think that God chose to bless Abraham and the Jewish nation at the expense of all the other nations of the earth. We tend to think in an either/or mentality. Either my nation is blessed or your nation is blessed. God has to choose one over the other. This is not at all the case. God clearly said to Abraham, "I will make of you a great nation and will bless you. I will make your name respected, and you will be a blessing. I will bless those who bless you, those who curse you I will curse; all the families of the earth will be blessed because of you" (Gen 12:2-3). This is a both/and promise. God chooses to bless Abraham in order that the nations of the world might be blessed in and through him. In one statement, God affirms the diversity of the people groups of the world while simultaneously unifying them with his blessing.

> Throughout the book, we will provide "Reflect" sections. Rather than consuming the information we are giving you as fast as you possibly can, stop and think and write and pray about these things. And discuss them with others. Bring others in your family, team, and staff, into your process. We believe you (and those you lead) will be better off as a result.

Reflect

How might the realization that God created the nations affect your perspectives on cultures, ethnicities, and diversity?

How could the awareness that all people on earth are somehow related affect your congregation's values and expressions?

Can you see how the disconnectedness of nations and individuals could be rooted in the either/or mentality?

Can you see how the both/and mentality highlights the fact that what is good for me is good for you because we are related? How can you promote this kind of both/and mentality in your congregation?

God Desires the Nations to Worship Him

There are many passages in Scripture (mostly in Psalms and Revelation, but sprinkled throughout as well) that call the nations to worship God. Psalm 46:10 tells us to be still and "know that I am God! I am exalted among all nations; I am exalted throughout the world!" The first part of this verse is quoted frequently in certain worship contexts, especially those that greatly value the practice of silence and stillness. But the second part of the verse is often overlooked. God desires to be exalted among the nations and in all the earth. Psalm 86:8-9 says plainly, "My Lord! There is no one like you among the gods! There is nothing that can compare to your works! All the nations that you've made will come and bow down before you, Lord; they will glorify your name." Notice that this verse reiterates that fact that it is God who made the people groups of the world. And the language here is *quite* inclusive. It says, "all" the nations God has made will worship him. It will happen. It is part of God's wise plan.

Reflect

Consider these scripture passages in addition to the ones cited above:

Psalm 45:17   Psalm 57:9   Psalm 67:3-4   Psalm 96:3-4

Psalm 117   Matthew 24:14   Revelation 15:3-4

Why do you think that is important to God that all nations worship him?

Why is it important that the gospel be preached to (and received by) all nations? Should this be important to us?

God Desires the Nations to Worship Him *Together*

Here is where it gets uncomfortable for many people. God's desire is not that we have our own separate worship services suited to our individual tastes and preferences. God's desire is not that our congregations be unified around language or culture, a common mission, a cool brand, a socioeconomic status, or a preferred musical style or worship approach.

In Revelation 7:9-10 we are given a glimpse of heaven. In it there is "a great crowd that no one could number. They were from every nation, tribe, people, and language. They were standing before the throne and before the Lamb. They wore white robes and held palm branches in their hands. They cried out with a loud voice: 'Victory belongs to our God who sits on the throne, and to the Lamb.'" God desires his people, from every nation (and in case we didn't understand that, it states even more explicitly, "from every nation, tribe, people, and nation") be unified around Jesus, worshipping together. Notice that there is not a Hispanic worship time at 9:00 a.m. around the throne while a Somali worship service happens somewhere else in heaven. All nations and tribes are together. In the same place and at the same time. As we consider that glimpse of heaven, let us consider the words of Jesus's prayer in Matthew 6:10: "Your kingdom come, your will be done, on earth as it is in heaven" (ESV). We don't know a lot about what heaven is like, but Scripture is clear that there will be multiethnic worship in heaven for eternity. And Jesus *himself* is praying for that to happen here on earth. Isn't that compelling enough for us to spend our lives praying for and working toward this vision of heaven on earth?

Notice that there is not a Hispanic worship time at 9:00 a.m. around the throne while a Somali worship service happens somewhere else in heaven. All nations and tribes are together. In the same place and at the same time.

God separated the nations at Babel but brought the nations together in Christ, at the cross. Consider Ephesians 2:14-16: "Christ is our peace. He made both Jews and Gentiles into one group. With his body, he broke down the barrier of hatred that divided us. He canceled the detailed rules of the Law so that he could create one new person out of the two groups, making peace. He reconciled them both as one body to God by the cross, which ended the hostility to God." *On the cross, God effectively dealt with everything that separates us from himself and from one another.* Sin and death are both formidable separators. But, on the cross, Jesus died to conquer both sin and death forever. He tore down the barrier, the dividing wall of hostility, and reconciled us to God, and in doing so, he made it possible as well for us to be reconciled to one another. Jesus himself is the Unifier, and he deserves to be the only Unifier of his Church.

In Acts 2, we see the flip side of what happened at the tower of Babel in Genesis 11. At Babel, people who the day before had been able to communicate with one another easily were suddenly not able to understand one another's speech. At Pentecost, people who that very morning had been separated by language were instantly able to understand one another because of the power of the Holy Spirit:

> When Pentecost Day arrived, they were all together in one place. Suddenly a sound from heaven like the howling of a fierce wind filled the entire house where they were sitting. They saw what seemed to be individual flames of fire alighting on each one of them. They were all filled with the Holy Spirit and began to speak in other languages as the Spirit enabled them to speak. There were pious Jews *from every nation under heaven* living in Jerusalem. When they heard this sound, a crowd gathered. They were mystified because *everyone* heard them speaking in their native languages. (Acts 2:1-6, emphasis added)

Notice that the text says that the people assembled that day were from "every nation under heaven." Is this any coincidence? Or is this yet another sign of God's heart for all the ethnic groups of the world? The church was born that day in a multiethnic environment. And so it continued. The church at Jerusalem was clearly multicultural as is evidenced by the cultural conflict that they experienced in Acts 6:1-7. One culture's widows were being treated well while another culture's widows were being overlooked. Note: the solution here, under the direction of the Holy Spirit, was to appoint culturally diverse, intentional leadership! The church at Antioch, where believers were first called Christians, was also clearly multicultural (see Acts 11:19-26).

Jesus himself, in an expression of righteous anger, addressed the issue of discrimination and cultural segregation in worship (among other things). You remember the scene. Jesus makes a whip and disrupts the buying and selling that was happening at the temple. You see, the merchants were selling sacrifices at ridiculous prices to non-Jews who would come from all over the world to the temple. In order to buy the sacrifices, the foreigners had to use local money. So the money changers got a piece of the action and made a profit off of the foreigners as well. The foreigners were being taken advantage of, and Jesus noticed. Also, tradition and archaeology tell us that the outer court of the temple was not really considered part of the temple. They also tell us that in order to enter the inner court, you had to walk up fourteen steps.

The Jewish Encyclopedia of 1906 tells us that at frequent intervals along these steps were signs in Greek and Latin that read, "No foreigner may pass within the lattice and wall around the sanctuary. Whoever is caught, the guilt for the death which will follow will be his own." After he overturned the tables of the money changers and the seats of those who sold pigeons, Jesus stood, most probably near one of these "keep out" signs, and said in Mark 11:17, "My house will be called a house of prayer for all nations." What does God desire? It seems pretty clear.

Reflect

Does your congregation seem to be unified around something other than Christ himself? If so, what? What could be done about that?

Can your congregation be accurately described as a "house of prayer for all the nations"? If not, why not?

Are you willing to pray along with Jesus for God's will to be done on earth as it is in heaven as it relates to multiethnic worship?

What would you be willing to do in order to bring that about?

Diverse or Dangerous?

If our worship is not diverse, it is dangerous.

Yes, I (Josh) know this is a strong statement. Yes, I know that in many churches all the worship leaders dress exactly alike and the band plays only one style of music throughout the service. Yes, I know that many churches are centered around one style of worship (free-flowing, liturgical, contemplative, and so on). But it has never been God's intention that only people who speak the same language or who come from the same culture or who like the same style of music should worship together. He wants his house to be a house of prayer for all nations. He intends for there to be diverse people worshipping together. And where there are diverse people, there are diverse expressions of worship. The Bible itself is full of diverse worship expressions. Standing up, sitting down, bowing down, laying prostrate, clapping hands, raising hands, shouting, silence, stillness, and dancing—it is easy to find all of these in scripture. Can they be found in your congregation? Here are some of the dangers you risk if the worship in your church is not diverse.

Danger #1: The Valuing of One Culture over Another

If you were to always order pizza with pepperoni on it and never order mushrooms on your pizza, it would be clear to me. Clearly, you value pepperoni more than mushrooms. You might get all philosophical about how you love pepperoni and mushrooms the same, but your practical decisions show what you truly value. And, therefore, what you don't value. For many of our churches, it is the same way with our worship services. We *say* we value every culture equally, but clearly, one language, one cultural way of doing things, and one style of music is dominant and obviously valued. And many others are not. Are you okay with this? Should you be?

> ### Reflect
> If a stranger were to walk into your worship services every week for a month, what would they be able to tell that you value?

Danger #2: The Judgment of One Culture as Right and Another as Wrong

This is actually a shorter leap than you might think from the first danger. These dangers exist on a slippery slope because inside all of us, there exists the strong belief that we are right and everyone else is, well, wrong. And many of us can wield Bible verses to support our positions. The Bible is largely silent on many of the things that people have such strong opinions about these days. Like the color of the carpet for instance. In fact, the Bible doesn't say anything about carpet or pews or giant screens or PowerPoint or whether a sermon should last for twenty minutes or two hours. It does not speak about whether the men and women should sit separately or if the music should have a B3 organ or an electric guitar. The Bible gives lots of freedom for the gospel to take root in a particular culture. And, therefore, the worship that results is a naturally distinct expression. Still, so many people have such strong opinions about these things that I (Josh) mentioned. And certain cultures express their opinions very freely.

I can't tell you how many times that I have heard a certain scripture quoted when cultures are crossing in the realm of worship. First Corinthians 14:40 says, quite simply, that "all things should be done decently and in order" (ESV). I will resist the urge to talk about how most people take this verse out of context. You can check that out for yourself. I will say this: most of the time when people quote this verse, they fail to realize that decency and order are cultural. What people are really saying in those situations is, "The way those people worship is not *my* view of decent or in *my* order." What is modest dress in the jungles of the Amazon may be considered immodest dress in the Middle East.

Let me (Josh) tell you about driving in the Dominican Republic. When my family moved to the Dominican Republic, one of the things that drove my dad crazy was the driving. To him, it seemed that there was no decency or order. The truth was, however, that the decency and order were vastly different from that of the United States. For example, in the United States, if there are two streets of approximately the same size, you would expect to see a stop sign or a traffic light at the place where these two streets intersect. In the Dominican Republic, this is not always the case. Often, there are two equal-sized streets that intersect and there are no visual cues as to who has the right of way. The procedure, which I have never seen written down anywhere (but everyone seems to know), is this: When you approach said intersection, you honk your car horn. If you hear a horn honk back, you stop at the intersection and then visually connect with the other driver to figure out who goes first. If you do not hear a horn honk back, then you are free to go through the intersection without stopping. You have the right of way. If your car horn isn't working, you fix it very quickly so you don't have to stop at every intersection! Now, my dad was pretty frustrated by the Dominican driving system. To be honest, it didn't feel much like a system to him. But there are some truly beautiful elements of the Dominican way of driving. Have you ever driven in the United States late at night in the middle of nowhere? Have you stopped at a traffic light and thought it was ridiculous you had to wait for two minutes for the light to turn green when there wasn't another car around for miles? The Dominicans have solved this problem. Be careful not to judge your worship expressions and forms as right and others around you as wrong.

Danger #3: The Failure to Engage Hearts

Our hearts are important to God. We are encouraged throughout the Bible to worship God with our whole hearts. And we are told in Ephesians 5 that we are to sing and make music in our hearts to the Lord. We will go into the concept of "heart music" more in depth in a later chapter, but for now let me say this. If worship in our church is not diverse, it will fail to engage hearts. For example, if you play only Southern gospel music every Sunday, some people will have their hearts engaged at a deep level by that music. Others will not. As worship leaders and pastors, we want the congregation's hearts to be engaged with God and with one another. If we only play one type of music, or if we always celebrate and never contemplate, we will only engage the hearts of one type of person. That's dangerous.

Danger #4: The Failure to Give God Glory

God is incredibly more diverse and more wonderful than his creation. Duane Elmer in the book *Cross-Cultural Conflict* writes:

> Diversity is rooted in the creative activity of God. But one wonders, why? For what reason did God display such variety in His human, plant, animal, and inorganic world? It is my conviction that only in this immense and grand variety could we begin to capture the character, grace, and glory of God. Put another way, God cannot adequately be revealed in a creation of similarities. ([Downers Grove, IL: Intervarsity Press, 1993], 23-24)

That last sentence is strong. If we are only a community of similarities, what do we reveal about God? And what do we fail to reveal about God? Unity in diversity is something far more wonderful than unity in similarity. Imagine a symphony. If all the different instruments were to play the same exact sounds and rhythms, it could be beautiful. But if all the different instruments were to play different and complementary sounds and rhythms, how much more beautiful it would be!

If we are only a community of similarities, what do we reveal about God? And what do we fail to reveal about God?

Danger #5: The Failure to Give an Accurate Picture of Christ to the World

For me, this is the most profound danger. Jesus, in John 17, prayed for the unity of all who would believe in him. (That includes you and me, by the way!)

> I'm not praying only for them but also for those who believe in me because of their word. I pray they will be one, Father, just as you are in me and I am in you. I pray that they also will be in us, so that the world will believe that you sent me. I've given them the glory that you gave me so that they can be one just as we are one. I'm in them and you are in me so that they will be made perfectly one. Then the world will know that you sent me and that you have loved them just as you loved me. (John 17:20-23)

Here, Jesus prays that all believers would be one, just as he is one with the Father. Think about that for a second. The Trinity (Father, Son, and Holy Spirit) is the perfect example of unity in diversity! They have always existed in diversity and in perfect community. There was at least one time in which the Son's will was in contrast to the Father's will. (Remember the prayer Jesus prayed before he was arrested?) So, even in diversity of opinions and desires, the Father and Son maintained perfect oneness. Jesus prays the same for us. We do not always need to agree in order to be one. But we must not let our disagreements divide us.

Jesus also prays that our oneness would be a witness to the world about who Jesus is. Our oneness will let the world know Jesus was sent by the Father and will testify of Jesus's love. What does our disunity communicate to the world about Jesus?

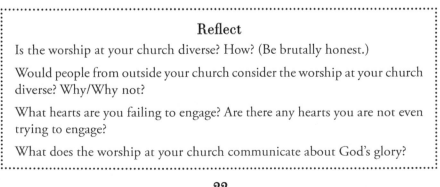

Reflect

Is the worship at your church diverse? How? (Be brutally honest.)

Would people from outside your church consider the worship at your church diverse? Why/Why not?

What hearts are you failing to engage? Are there any hearts you are not even trying to engage?

What does the worship at your church communicate about God's glory?

A Better Way

There is a real tendency in our world today to make worship all about us. How many times have you heard someone say, "Worship was great today!" and then when you ask why, it is simply because they got to sing their favorite songs, hear something inspiring, and weren't distracted by any major technical malfunctions? I (Josh) am afraid that we as worship leaders can cater to the consumer mind-set of many church members. We try to please people, and in doing so, we unwittingly communicate that worship is about them. For years, after leading worship on Sunday mornings, I would have a line of people waiting to give me feedback about the service. The feedback usually fell into these two categories: (1) I liked something we did in worship today, and I want to do more of it, or (2) I didn't like something about worship today, and I don't want us to do that again. My guess is that many of you have experienced the same type of feedback. I would be okay with that feedback from people who don't know and follow Jesus. But I believe Jesus offers us the example and opportunity for a better way.

> Therefore, if there is any encouragement in Christ, any comfort in love, any sharing in the Spirit, any sympathy, complete my joy by thinking the same way, having the same love, being united, and agreeing with each other. Don't do anything for selfish purposes, but with humility think of others as better than yourselves. Instead of each person watching out for their own good, watch out for what is better for others. (Phil 2:1-4)

Our natural tendency is to watch out for our own good. Our natural tendency is to think of ourselves more highly than others. We are encouraged to be like Jesus, however, by, *in humility*, thinking of others as better than ourselves. What if, instead of the line of people ready to tell me what they want more/less of for themselves, this were to happen:

- A gentleman from Ethiopia says, "I noticed we sang a lot of songs in Amharic today! And I love singing in my language! But I also noticed we didn't sing any songs in Spanish. My friend Lucas speaks Spanish, and when we sing in his language, it really touches his heart. Could we sing something in Spanish next week?"

23

- A Hispanic grandmother says, "I don't really get the loud electric guitar stuff and the American rock 'n' roll sound. But that really is important to my grandson. Thanks for playing music like that today. I loved watching my grandson lift his hands in worship this morning!"

The truth is, that as followers of Jesus, we should be more concerned with one another than we are with ourselves. I should fight for *you*. And you should fight for *me*. I should stand up for you. And you should make sure that I am cared for. In many of our congregations, however, people don't know one another well enough to be able to care for one another. They don't know what each other's preferences are to be able to fight for them. That is a problem. And it is one reason why we need to find ways to develop worshipping communities and not simply worship experiences.

Reflect

How can you help cultivate an attitude of "preferring one another" in your congregation?

What opportunities could you make for people to know one another in your congregation?

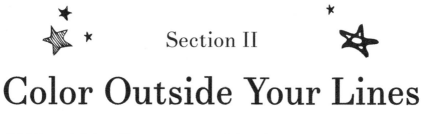

Section II

Color Outside Your Lines

[Life within diverse worshipping communities]

Chapter 3

Worshipping Communities or Worship Experiences?

Are we to be about more than simply structuring worship experiences?
We are designed for relationships. We are called to belong in worshipping
communities.

A few years ago, our friend Jaewoo Kim, a Korean missionary and cross-cultural leader, posed a thought-provoking question to a group of multicultural worship leaders who had gathered together to seek God. He asked, "Is our goal to facilitate worship experiences or to develop worshipping communities?" In other words, is what we do as worship leaders about helping people have moments of engagement with God? Or is it about engaging not only with God but also with one another? Is it our aim to structure worship centers that are beautiful and worship services that run smoothly without any glitches? Or is it to allow people to be built together like living stones into a spiritual temple? There is a vast difference between the two.

Is our goal to facilitate worship experiences or to develop worshipping communities?
—Jaewoo Kim

Let's be clear. Worship experiences are not bad. They are indeed good. But they aren't enough. It is too small a goal, too short-sighted a vision to simply desire to facilitate worship experiences.

Worship experiences are temporary. Worshipping communities are eternal. Worship experiences are individual. Worshipping communities are individuals coming together in diversity and unity. Worship experiences are about the worship. Worshipping communities are about more than just the worship. Worship experiences can be controlled. Worshipping communities are shepherded. Worshipping communities have worship experiences. But worship experiences do not necessarily lead to worshipping communities.

Worshipping communities have worship experiences. But worship experiences do not necessarily lead to worshipping communities.

Eternal Community

Community has always existed. Before time began, God was. Father, Son, and Holy Spirit have always existed. Unity. Diversity. Perfect community. Jesus says in John 17:5 that he shared glory with the Father before the creation of the world. And in the process of God creating, we see the Trinity functioning together beautifully. The Father created according to Malachi 2. The Spirit brooded upon the waters in Genesis 1. God spoke and everything that is came to be, by the power of his Word. Jesus himself is the Word of God according to John 1. When it came time to create people, God said, "Let *us* make humanity in our image to resemble *us*" (Gen 1:26, emphasis added). We are made in the image of an "us." We are created in the image of a diverse yet unified community. God is a diverse yet unified community.

We are made in the image of an "us."

It is our belief that in order to more fully reflect God's glory, we (the church) must be what, in Christ, we already are, that is, diverse and unified. Let's break that down.

<u>*We are the fullness of Christ.*</u> Ephesians 1:23 says that Jesus's body, the church, "is the fullness of Christ, who fills everything in every way." The church is the fullness of Christ. No one person is the fullness of Christ on her own. But the church together, the community, is the fullness of Christ.

<u>*We are to reflect God's glory.*</u> "All of us are looking with unveiled faces at the glory of the Lord as if we were looking in a mirror. We are being transformed into that same image from one degree of glory to the next degree of glory. This comes from the Lord, who is the Spirit" (2 Cor 3:18). As we look at the glory of the Lord *together* (some would say this is a good definition of worship), we *together* are being transformed into the likeness of God in ever-increasing glory.

<u>*We are diverse.*</u> Take the time to read through 1 Corinthians 12 and Romans 12 to see how God intends for there to be variety in the church. Romans 12:4-5 says it well: "We have many parts in one body, but the parts don't all have the same function. In the same way, though there are many of us, we are one body in Christ, and individually we belong to each other."

<u>*We are unified in Christ.*</u> "You are all God's children through faith in Christ Jesus. All of you who were baptized into Christ have clothed yourselves with Christ. There is neither Jew nor Greek; there is neither slave nor free; nor is there male and female, for you are all one in Christ Jesus" (Gal 3:26-28). According to Ephesians 4:3 we have already been given the Spirit of unity. It is not our job to make unity happen. Rather, it is our job to preserve the unity we already have in Christ.

It is not our job to make unity happen. Rather, it is our job to preserve the unity we already have in Christ.

The reality is that community has always existed in God. We have been created in the image of that community. We have been invited into and saved into community. We are a reflection of that community. And we will be part of a worshipping community for eternity. Revelation chapters 5 and 7 give us a glimpse of that reality. We see a picture of people from every tribe and language worshipping around the throne of God together. We will be singing, shouting, and bowing down together for eternity with the redeemed from every nation and every age. What an experience that will be! But not just an experience. What a community that will be!

Reflect

Do our worship gatherings here on earth prepare us for what is to come?

As a worship leader, how are you preparing your congregation to stand before God's throne?

In what ways are you preparing them to stand before God's throne *together with all the saints*?

The Importance of Relationships

Our relationships are important to God. From Genesis to Revelation, the Bible speaks to us about the importance of relationships. When God created Adam, he put him in a garden. Every evening God would come to the garden to walk and share with Adam. When sin broke the relationship between God and people, God sent his only son, Jesus, to pay the punishment for sin so that relationship might be restored. We were designed to live in intimate relationship with God. But notice, that even when Adam was living in perfect relationship with God (before sin entered the world), it was not enough. God noticed that Adam was alone and that wasn't a good thing. We were designed to have meaningful relationships with others as well.

It is impossible to separate our relationship with God from our relationships with others:

> We love because God first loved us. If anyone says, I love God, and hates a brother or sister, he is a liar, because the person who doesn't love a brother or sister who can be seen can't love God, who can't be seen. This commandment we have from him: Those who claim to love God ought to love their brother and sister also. (1 John 4:19-21)

Our relationships with others affect our relationship with God. It is ridiculous to claim that you love God but harbor prejudice about someone who is made in God's image. We are fooling ourselves if we believe that we can have amazing worship experiences with God if our relationships are not right in our worshipping community. Relationships are important to God! So important, that Matthew 5:23-24 tells us to leave our gift at the altar and go be reconciled with a brother if something isn't right in one of our relationships. What might that look like in today's worship services? Let's imagine an extreme example. Can you envision a singer on the worship team putting his microphone down in the middle of a song? Imagine him leaving the stage and finding someone in the congregation to ask for their forgiveness. Can you picture the drummer putting her drumsticks down in the middle of a worship set and excusing herself to go make a phone call to an estranged family member? Some might argue that such behavior could ruin the worship experience for other people. Ah, but what is more important: the worship experience or the worshipping community? If a drummer delays reconciliation for the sake of the "worship experience," she declares that the worship experience is more important than the worshipping community. If a worship leader harbors bitterness toward a pastor but continues to sing and pray as if nothing is wrong, what does that say about the value of the worshipping community? Could the act of reconciling with another be a worship experience in itself?

In John 4, we read a conversation that Jesus had with a Samaritan woman. She was questioning what worship should look like. Should it happen here or there? It reminds me of some worship-planning meetings I have been a part of in the past. Should there be a prayer before or after this song? Should we have everyone stand or sit? There is no end, it seems, to those kinds of questions. Jesus responds to her question by saying that the Father is looking for worshippers who will worship in spirit and truth. God is not merely seeking worship. God is seeking people who will worship him. God is not looking for the right song to be sung in the right key with the perfect arrangement. God is looking for hearts of people that are inclined to worship him.

Reflect

By the way we spend our time and our energy, people can tell what we value.

By the choices we make, people can determine what is important to us.

By the way you spend your time, are you showing that you are more concerned with worship experiences or with worshipping communities?

By the choices you are making, are you demonstrating that you are as concerned with your relationships as God is?

Are you investing in the lives of worshippers as much as you are preparing for the practical nuts and bolts of a worship service?

Why Is This Relevant?

If you are unwilling to address the pride and ethnocentrism in your heart, you will do more harm than good in your efforts to lead multicultural worship. If you are not willing to help people in your congregation deal with the prejudices in their own hearts and relationships, multicultural worship will never work. What good is it if people can sing a song in someone else's language if they don't truly love that person? Isn't it kind of like a resounding gong or a clanging symbol? What good is it if diverse people sit in the same pew week after week but couldn't care less about one another? What good is it if everyone sings a song perfectly in tune but their hearts are in constant dissonance with one another? What good are our best worship experiences if they don't help us be more like the worshipping community we were redeemed to be?

Multicultural worship without honest, authentic, cross-cultural relationships is offensive. Did you know that if you introduce a song in Spanish in a worship service, it can actually dishonor the Hispanics in your midst? Let's say you misspell a word in Spanish or mispronounce a syllable. (These things are bound to happen when you are learning a new language, by the way.) If you have no relationship with people and no humility in your heart, those things can actually be hurtful. People might think, "That worship leader is just trying to appease us by singing a song in our language, but she didn't even take the time to get it right." Or, "Why is he teaching the Spanish pronunciation as if he knows? He is doing it all wrong!" However, if a worship leader is building authentic cross-cultural relationships with Latinos and humbly trying her best to sing in Spanish, those same misspellings and mispronunciations might actually make her more endearing to the Hispanics in the congregation.

Let's say you look out in your congregation and see that there are several Black families in attendance. If you incorporate your best attempt at a Black gospel song next Sunday, you can actually alienate the very people you are trying to reach. It is entirely possible that those Black families in your congregation are not African American at all. Maybe they are Jamaican and could be grieved that you didn't take the time to find out their ethnicity. Or maybe they are African American people who don't like gospel music. (I have a number of friends like that!) Without taking the time to really get to know people, all you are left with is your assumptions about them, based on stereotypes and partial information and previous experiences. This can be dangerous!

> Without taking the time to really get to know people, all you are left with is your assumptions about them, based on stereotypes and partial information and previous experiences.

I am often asked about how to avoid tokenism in multicultural worship. My answer is quite simple. If the song (or any service element) is disconnected from authentic relationship, it can feel like tokenism. The same action can be interpreted as kindness or tokenism, depending on the presence or absence of mutual respect and relationship!

> The same action can be interpreted as kindness or tokenism, depending on the presence or absence of mutual respect and relationship!

Consideration, Not Quotas

Dr. David A. Anderson, in his book *Gracism: The Art of Inclusion*, defines the term *racism* as "speaking, acting or thinking negatively about someone else solely based on that person's color, class or culture" ([Downers Grove, IL: Intervarsity Press, 2007], 21). Given that definition, Anderson has coined the new term, combining the word *racism* with the word *grace* (God's unmerited favor), gracism. He defines *gracism* as "the positive extension of favor on other humans based on color, class, or culture." The term *gracism* has become one of my most favorite terms to use when trying to describe what intentional multicultural ministry looks like. How do we avoid tokenism? Gracism.

We avoid racial tokenism through relationships. We also avoid tokenism through how we think (our mind-sets) and how we communicate (what we say). When Josh and I (Nikki) travel around to speak on issues of diversity and multicultural ministry, we often hear concerns from leaders about being so intentional. Why should we actually go after someone or choose someone to be a part of things because of his or her race? Isn't that in itself a form of racism? Well, not according to Anderson's definition of racism. Racism has a *negative* association, while being intentional about including someone because of his or her ethnicity has a *positive* association. What we are talking about in this book is being intentional about including people and making room for people within your ministry based on their ethnicity, culture, and background. This concept can feel a little uncomfortable if you are not used to thinking about ethnicity and race in positive terms. Intentionality, however, should never be mistaken for some sort of racial quota system or affirmative action plan for the people of God. It goes much deeper than that. What we are talking about here is *consideration*, not *quotas*.

Quotas are used to measure numbers and ratios. Quotas are used when you want to figure out "how many" of something that you have. Quotas are useful when you are meeting budget numbers, counting members in an organization, or quantifying stock numbers. Quotas should never enter the question when we are talking about people, especially when we are talking about people within our multicultural ministry. A mind-set based on quotas is dangerous for those already leading or even beginning to lead in a multicultural environment. Quotas lead to scheduling a vocal team based solely on how many different races of people you have on your team and, if one is missing, looking for a replacement based on the fact that you just need "one of them," whatever "one of them" represents. A mind-set based on quota systems does not consider that people are actually *people* who have something to offer. A mind-set based on quota systems prompts a leader to say such things as, "We need a White person on stage this week," or "We need to make sure that we have a woman on the stage." Quotas in multicultural ministry are dangerous and lead us to think of people as objects, so that we can claim that we are diverse when in fact all we have done is provide ethnic window dressing and devalued our people in the process.

Quotas in multicultural ministry are dangerous and lead us to think of people as objects, so that we can claim that we are diverse when in fact all we have done is provide ethnic window dressing and devalued our people in the process.

Consideration is something that the Apostle Paul talks about in 1 Corinthians 12. Paul has a conversation about how the body of Christ is like a physical body—one body, many parts. Each part has its own special function and its own importance. Some of the parts are more dignified than others. Some of the parts need special honor, extra care, and consideration. He says in verses 24 through 26: "But God has put the body together, giving greater honor to the part with less honor so that there won't be division in the body and so the parts might have mutual concern for each other. If one part suffers, all the parts suffer with it; if one part gets the glory, all the parts celebrate with it." This sounds *much* more acceptable than quota systems. Paul is talking about the idea of consideration and honor. Equal concern. This is the mind-set of consideration, not quotas. A mind-set of consideration allows us to see people as people and what their ethnic heritage and cultures bring to our communities rather than see just skin color, which makes us feel good about what we see with our own eyes.

Consideration says we need that person in our community because *we are just better and fuller as a community when we are as diverse as we can be!* It is the hand saying to the foot, "I need you." It is the eye saying to the stomach, "I need you." It is the heart saying to the pinky toe, "I need you." Can you imagine how our strut would be without a pinky toe? *That* is the fruit of consideration! That is how you avoid making people within your ministries feel like they are tokens in your ministry game. Why do you need a White person on your team? Because when he is present, he brings a cultural richness to the group. Why do you need a Spanish speaker on your team? Because when she is present, she gives others a glimpse into their cultural beauty. Why do you need an African American on your team? Because he brings all of his own cultural experiences that add to this beautiful tapestry that is being woven together within our multicultural ministry. This is consideration, not quotas. Doesn't this way of thinking just feel good and more freeing? Isn't it much better to see people as human and full of ideas, experiences, and cultural beauty rather than simply filling a gap or a need in your plan?

Reflect

In what ways have you been operating on assumptions rather than taking the time to get to know people?

Who can you reach out to now in an effort to know them better? (Put the book down. Make that phone call. Write that e-mail. Go have that cup of coffee with someone. Then come back!)

What are two things that you can do this week to consider those of another ethnicity within your ministry? How might you be able to help them see the value they add to the team because of their ethnic heritage?

Practical Ways to Develop Worshipping Communities (Not Just Worship Experiences)

A few years ago, I (Josh) had the opportunity to preach at a local Christian school chapel. This Christian school has a good number of international students, mostly from China and South Korea. As I planned and prepared for that opportunity, I prayed that God would help me do something that would develop the worshipping community at that school. A few days after the chapel, I got the chance to speak with one of the international students. He said, "Chapel was good this week." I smiled and then probed, "What was good about it?" He paused and then in broken English said, "It improved our relationships." When I asked what he meant, he said that since the chapel, he feels like the American students understand the international students better and are more apt to engage in conversation with them. I was blown away. God was clearly at work. I stopped to consider what I did practically that helped facilitate this answer to my prayers. Here are some helpful principles:

1. *Think long-term instead of short-term.* How could what you do in the worship service this Sunday last beyond the length of the service? How could you do something in the one hour you have together as a congregation that will improve their relationships with one another? I chose to use my influence as a guest speaker to ask the student-led worship team to sing the chorus of a popular American worship song in Chinese and Korean. I sent them the words ahead of time and arrived early to help them rehearse. I knew that trying to sing a song in a different language would help them understand how the international students feel every week singing in English. I hoped this might make them more open to considering singing songs in other languages after I was gone.

2. *Learn to be okay with messiness.* I asked students to read the scripture for that morning in different languages. Some of them stumbled through the readings. It was not flawless or seamless. There were moments of awkward laughter, but we also got to hear Chinese students who had never been on stage before reading the scripture beautifully in their own language. If there is no room for messiness in your worship gatherings, then there is no room for people who don't have it all together (which is all of us, by the way!). If there is no room for anything less than excellence, then people who may have a unique skill or language can't leverage it unless they are professional speakers, singers, or readers. If you avoid awkwardness and discomfort, you will never have to be humble, because you only choose to do things that you know you can do well.

3. *Find ways to get the focus off the stage.* Most times, in our worship gatherings, the focus is on the stage. If someone leads in prayer, that person comes up on stage. If someone gives a testimony, she comes up on stage. If someone gives announcements, he comes up on stage. There can be a sense that anything that is officially part of the worship service happens on stage. Many times, as worship leaders, we recognize that people need to connect with God and with us. But we forget the importance of them connecting with one another. It is hard for them to do that, if they are

always facing the stage. At best, they are only ever in one another's peripheral view, if they can see one another at all (depending on the lighting!) They never get to focus on one another. In this chapel service, I had people who had lived in other countries stand up. I asked them simply to say what country they had lived in. It was simple. But it was amazing! People learned things they never knew about one another. Some people had lived in the same country at the same time and didn't know it until that opportunity. Greeting time can be a good way for people to focus on one another. Also, why not ask a question and have them turn to someone and talk about it for a minute? It's a great way for them to engage with one another. And, who knows? That minute of conversation might lead to a real, authentic relationship after the worship service ends.

Reflect

List three practical ways you can help get the focus off the stage during worship.

1.

2.

3.

List three practical things you can do in a worship service that could help people improve their relationships with one another.

1.

2.

3.

There Are People Out There!

I (Nikki) visited a church once on a Sunday evening. Being someone who loves the experience of corporate worship, I was looking forward to being led. The worship team and its leader came out onto the platform in front of the crowd. The man stepped up to the microphone and said, "Stand and worship with us." There was no "hello," no "glad you are here," no "is there anyone new?" Really? The worship team on the stage then proceeded to move through the entire worship set without saying anything else to "the room" or to me as someone in the room. At the end of the set, the man said, "You can have your seat." That's it? Now, I totally understand this may be a personal preference issue on my part, but I was turned off by the experience. Was I able to have my own worship moment with Jesus? Of course. I'm a big girl and mature enough to find my way to worship, but there was something innately *human* missing from this moment. It was the lack of engagement.

One of the best things you bring to worship when you are in front of people is not your songs or your music, but it is you and how you reveal the character of Christ through how he has made you. I love the admonition in 1 John 4:12: "No one has ever seen God. If we love each other, God remains in us and his love is made perfect in us."

That scripture blows my mind. There is something powerful and wonderful that happens when believers gather together in the same space, the same room. God's love is brought to full expression. John says that it is like we are seeing the living God in the flesh right before our eyes. You do not cease to be a person once you step on a stage, a platform, or in front of someone while leading in worship. You bring parts of yourself and who you are. You are not a robot, and that's a good thing!

It felt awkward to be a visitor at that church and feel like the people on stage didn't care if I was in the room. Because we were not even acknowledged, it felt like we were not considered an integral part of the holy moment that was taking place. What makes corporate worship so unique and powerful? Is it the spirit of Jesus? Yes. However, Jesus is present with us each individually wherever we are. If I wanted to worship by myself without human interaction, why did I even leave my house and drive for an hour? Our engaging with one another in the presence of God is part of what makes a corporate worship experience so powerful. Don't underestimate the influence you have for Christ in your role and position. Connect with and engage the people you lead with yourself, with each other, and with God every time you have the opportunity to be in front of them. In the American context, many nondominant cultures (non-White) thrive on such opportunities to engage with one another. Worship is a community experience filled with expression, conversation, agreements, and laughter.

Connect with and engage the people you lead with yourself, with each other, and with God every time you have the opportunity to be in front of them.

Now, you will need to be familiar with your own church culture and context as well as your own personality (which we will address in upcoming chapters), but here are a few practical ideas on how to engage with people as you lead worship:

- Acknowledge people in the room, corporately and individually.

- Tell stories of songs or stories from your community.

- Give your audience verbal cues throughout worship of the road map of the songs. Verbally tell them where you are leading them.

- Encourage people along the way: "you've got it!"; "you sound beautiful!"

- Laugh together. If something funny or entertaining happens during worship, make it a shared experience.

- Use "we" language when speaking during worship. The use of terms such as *we, us,* and *our* helps your congregation realize the truth of our unity in Christ.

- Help people get to know one another by gathering diverse groups of people and asking them questions.

Beyond the Worship Service

Your leadership does not just happen when you are on stage. You don't have to have a microphone in your hand to be a leader. You are a leader beyond the worship service. A first step for you as a worship leader might be to get diverse (generations, cultures, and so on) people together in a nonthreatening environment. Food is always good. Once you get them there, ask them to take turns answering some questions like:

1. What is one song that really helps you connect with God in worship? And why?
2. What part of the worship service is the most meaningful to you? And why?

This kind of gathering is helpful on so many levels. First, some people will never share these things (or even think about them) unless they are given the opportunity by someone in leadership. Second, people can learn the vital skill of listening to one another. Third, stereotypes will be broken down as people give answers that will surprise others. Last, church members will learn about one another's preferences, which is the first step toward preferring others above themselves.

Our Prayer for You

[We] kneel before the Father. Every ethnic group in heaven or on earth is recognized by him. [We] ask that he will strengthen you in your inner selves from the riches of his glory through the Spirit. [We] ask that Christ will live in your hearts through faith. As a result of having strong roots in love, [we] ask that you'll have the power to grasp love's width and length, height and depth, together with all believers. [We] ask that you'll know the love of Christ that is beyond knowledge so that you will be filled entirely with the fullness of God. Glory to God, who is able to do far beyond all that we could ask or imagine by his power at work within us; glory to him in the church and in Christ Jesus for all generations, forever and always. Amen. (Eph 3:14-21)

Chapter 4

Integrate Yourself

You are not just a leader. You are a whole person. You are an important part of something much bigger than yourself. Treat yourself like it.

You Are Not a Superhero

I know, I know, I (Nikki) just crushed your dreams, aspirations, and any faulty hope that you may have been holding onto that at some point in the near future you would be able to wear those light blue tights and red bloomers on stage during your worship set. My bad, but it's true. And the sooner that you and I embrace this truth, the more freedom we may actually be able to experience. We have weaknesses. We have frailties. We have things that trip us up. We are human. One of the most common pitfalls for leaders (especially church leaders) is segregation. That's right, that's what I said. Strong word, right? Segregation. To separate oneself. To isolate oneself. It's an awful word, really. Unless you are talking about laundry. Then trust me, it's always good to segregate reds and whites.

I cannot tell you how many times people have told me (referring to leadership) that it's lonely at the top. Segregate. Be careful who you trust. Segregate. You can't let everybody in. Segregate. And while I do believe that we need to be wise in the relationships that we choose (when it is in our power to choose them), what can happen to us is that we go all the way to the extreme in our segregations and subconsciously decide that we do not need the same things that the humans around us need. That we are, indeed, superhuman. We subconsciously believe that we can just fly around town with our capes and our shields saving the world, lifting buses off of grandmothers, getting cats out of trees, and waking up the next day to do it all again. Do you ever notice in the movies that we never see the superheroes needing anything or anyone? Exactly. That's not you. Because you are like me—human. You need deep relationships. You need people who truly know you and can challenge you. You need to engage in activities because you love them and not because they are just what's best for the church or ministry that you lead. If you are completely focused on the people who need you and their preferences, you slowly cease to become a person. But you are a person. A whole person. Every area of your life is important to God. And your talents, leadership, health, habits, heart, soul, and mind are all connected, whether we try to segregate them or not.

Superheroes Don't Need Friends

Because you are a real human and not a superhero, you need to allow people in your world to love you and know your heart. It is easy to start believing somewhere along the line that you can't have real relationships and real friends because of your role in church leadership. This can seem like wisdom, but it is not. Many times this idea is fostered by leaders who have become jaded and burned by past relationships. It is possible (in some weird innocently subconscious way) to decide that it isn't a good idea to allow the worlds of church leadership and church members to mix. All the while, in your heart, if you are honest, you have a longing to belong. You see people gather together for birthdays and barbeques, and you want to gather with them and share real relationship. But you wrestle with fear. "What if they see who I really am? Would they still follow me? Would they be disappointed? Would they get tired of me?" What if, instead of doubting the longing of your heart to belong, you started doubting your fears more?

One of the roles that I, as a worship leader, love the most is caring for the hearts and helping steward the emotional baggage of those who I lead. For me to lean into my work and realize that the decisions I make are for the benefit of the community is a responsibility that I take great joy in. But I must remember to include myself as a part of that community. And you must, too. The community that you are creating within your churches and ministries for those who you lead is the very same community that you get to be a part of as well. So, integrate yourself as a part of that community. Integrate yourself into the community instead of acting like you are above it.

We were created for relationship, and our relationships are important to God. The role of the multicultural worship leader is to develop multicultural worshipping communities rather than simply to design diverse worship experiences. How can you develop community if you have no community yourself? How can you encourage the people you lead to invest in real relationships across cultural and language barriers if you are not investing in those yourself? What might it look like to be integrated as a leader of a multicultural community? Does it look different for someone who leads in primarily mono-ethnic communities? Dr. David Anderson, pastor of Bridgeway Community Church, has a brilliant saying. He says, "A multicultural ministry begins with a multicultural lifestyle." Start to live it before you try and lead it. Don't segregate yourself from the people you lead.

> # "A multicultural ministry begins with a multicultural lifestyle."
> # —Dr. David Anderson

Multicultural worship leaders are always looking for opportunities to build relationship with diverse people. It is one of the most important things that we can do, particularly in diverse environments. Without relationships with people who are different than us, ethnically, we set ourselves up for assumptions, accusations, and skepticism toward others, and we can invite those same things onto ourselves. A leader trying to build a multicultural lifestyle is intentional about building relationships outside of her own race. For instance, when I (Nikki) was looking for a new doctor a year or so ago, the first question I asked myself wasn't, "How can I find the best doctor"; my question was, "Who is missing from my life?" I had realized that I had no one speaking into my life who was from Indian descent. Not that I didn't have friends who were of Indian heritage, but I had no authority figure in my life who I could receive from. What better way to have someone direct the course of my life than to look for an accomplished Indian doctor? Let me be clear, I didn't look for an Indian doctor so that I could check it off of my list of diverse friends—no, that is a quota system. I looked for this person because I believed that he or she could add a perspective to my life that I did not already have. That person's influence in my life would help me grow as a person and learn.

Where do you get your hair cut? Who does your taxes? Who is your doctor or your florist? What restaurants do you frequent? Who is your dry-cleaner? Who is your child's tutor? Who works on your car? These are all areas in which we may be able to build relationships with people who are different than us. Go where the people are!

Superheroes Don't Need Food

Recognizing the reality that you are human, give yourself permission to fall back in love with music and art. You have been designed by God as a creative person. It is one way you are made in God's image. As worship leaders and pastors and tech people and praise band members, however, it is easy to get so caught up with the nuts and bolts of the music, the lighting, the theme, and so on, that we lose our passion for beauty and artistic creativity. It is easy to read Scripture and listen to music and even shop for clothes all the while wearing your analytical "work hat." You may fall into the trap, like I have, of only listening to music through the filter of whether you could sing it and pull it off at church. You may always be asking the question, "Is it right for our congregation?" There is nothing inherently wrong with this, but if you are not careful, you will forget how to just listen and love music and art simply for the pure joy of it. Maybe you already have. It is important to feed your creative side and to make opportunities for yourself to simply enjoy the goodness and beauty of art. Many of us have friends who have gone to seminary, and somewhere around year two or three these friends who had entered seminary or Bible school with a zeal for ministry and a passion for God's word have lost the desire because they begin to study the Bible as a textbook and look at ministry through the lens of "work" instead of allowing these things to continue to influence their own lives and stories. They forget how to feed themselves. If you are a creative person—musician, vocalist, artist, dancer, painter, graphic artist, videographer, or photographer—be intentional to feed yourself. You are human, and you need creative nourishment.

Get life in order to give life. I had to embrace this in order to survive within the community and as a leader. There are ways that I had to pursue in order to feed myself so I could feed others. There is a reason why flight attendants on an airplane tell you to put the oxygen mask on yourself before you try to help others. Who knew the airline industry could make us aware of such a beautiful life principle? You cannot give life if you do not have life to give. You cannot give what you do not possess. If you run out of life you cannot give it. Don't fool yourself.

The challenge is that most of our lives are full. Full of really good things. We have choices to make. And for many of us, we are not making a choice between robbing a bank and going to worship rehearsal. We are choosing between coffee with a struggling friend and a gig at the bar down the street. But we cannot continue to run on fumes. You must care for and steward yourself in order to lead effectively. Remember that *you matter, too.* We are our best selves when we are feeding ourselves. Don't you get grumpy when you don't eat?

Do not settle for the segregation of your heart and your soul. Even Jesus needed relationships and rest. If it was good enough for him being fully man as well as fully God, then why do we think we do not need it? It is a good discipline to care for people and to consider others better than yourself, but we also need to realize that our own souls need care, too. Don't forget that you are a person, too. And just as you care for others, you need to be cared for as well. You are a part of that community of people.

Practical Ways to Feed Your Creative Soul

Most of you reading this book are Creatives. You are people who love art and music and dance. You love symphonies and films and show tunes. Yes, show tunes. You could read ten books on leadership and stewardship of your own soul if you were a "normal" person. But let's be honest. If you are a Creative, then you are not normal, and neither am I. Since that is the case, embrace the fact that you may need something completely different when it comes to the stewardship of your creative self. Lean into it, not away from it. Trust me, you will feel more alive and true to yourself than you have felt in the past, you will grow as a leader, and the people you lead will thank you. Here are some ideas for nurturing your creative soul.

1. Find out what you love and don't judge it; just do it.

One of the most freeing things you can do is give yourself to the things that you love just because you love them. Not because it's good for your church community or your nonprofit or anyone else around you, but because it breathes life into you as an artist and a person. What do you love to do? You have been created a very specific way and for very specific things. The Bible says that you have been made "fearfully and wonderfully" (Ps 139:14 ESV) If that is the case and you have been made uniquely, then chances are that what nourishes you and makes you a creative person will be different than the things that nourish your executive pastor (unless the pastor is a Creative, too, and then maybe you both should go see a Broadway show together).

The reality is that sometimes we just need permission to be ourselves and love the things that we love just because we love them. At times it is so much safer for us to just look at the lives of others whom we perceive as having it all together and to try to figure out what it is that they are doing and then copy and paste it into our own worlds. If we are not careful, we can even subconsciously use these things as a litmus test and use this criteria to develop a sense that God may be pleased with us. When we do this, it keeps us living a safe life and embracing a perception that we will live our lives without failure because if it looks like it worked for the person next to us, then it must be the right thing to do. Unfortunately, this can keep us from being courageous and finding our own path. So, what is it that you love? What is that thing that you have been thinking about since I asked the question? What is it that the people around you may think is a little crazy or a waste of time? Do you love it? Yeah, do that. In fact, stop reading this chapter and do it right now.

2. Expand your creative horizons and learn from diverse people.

Just because you are not in school anymore doesn't mean that you have to stop learning and challenging yourself, creatively. When is the last time that you have gone to a conference hosted by a church that is made up of a different ethnicity than you? When is the last time that you read a theology or music book written by someone who is different from you, ethnically? Hopefully you can remember, but if you can't, this is what we are talking about. Multicultural worship leaders are intentionally trying to learn from other ethnic groups how they see the world around them, how they interpret the words of Jesus, and the insight that they have on how to do ministry. It is one the greatest resources multicultural leaders have available to them.

Listen to music. Lots of it. Remember when you used to study all kinds of music as opposed to just listening to latest, "hottest" corporate worship song? Listen to music across cultures and genres. Be curious about music without fear. If you haven't listened to classical music in a while, grab a disc of Chopin Nocturnes. Are Black gospel artists the only people on your iPod? Go out and find some Contemporary Christian Music (CCM) Rock Worship Music and find out what those musicians are doing. Is it all funk music all the time? Go out and listen to some bluegrass or something from the Middle East. Download some worship music in the Hindi language. Whatever it is, go listen to it. My husband, who is an incredible drummer, always says, "You are what you listen to." I love that quote, and it's true. If you want to steward your creative, musical soul, listen to lots of music. If you are not sure where to start, just ask people what they are listening to. Listen to music that you wouldn't normally try out. It will expand your mind. Listening to an array of musical genres will also inform your own musical style and allow it to develop.

Likewise, go see films. All kinds. Documentaries, "shoot-'em-ups," tear-jerkers, chick flicks, and comedies. I guarantee you will love some and hate the others. But your creative and cultural horizons will have expanded!

3. Rest a lot, eat well, celebrate often, and repeat weekly.

Here is the deal: We all need to sleep at some point; that is just a given. Remember, you are not a superhero, so you will need to go to sleep at some point. Depending on your definition, sleep and rest can be two different things or the same thing. This is up to you to determine. What helps you delight in God? What centers your mind back on him and the plans that he has for you? Your answers will determine what rest looks like for you. Schedule it just like you would schedule a meeting you had at work and prioritize your time. If you are a beginner in allowing yourself rest, it may not happen unless you plan for it. Schedule time for rest, particularly around holidays. Easter and Christmas. Crazy times, right? Oftentimes we run ourselves into the ground. We will work normal work hours and then tack on an extra five hours. Who is asking us to do this? Where can we take some time off? If this is impossible, can we talk to our leaders to get some extended time? Or, what might need to be put on the back burner during the holidays so that when the holidays are over, we are poured out, not completely burned out. Know what is important in a given season of life.

Eat well. Why? Because your body is a gift, a gift given to you on loan from God. Your body is his. Therefore, we cannot just treat it like it doesn't matter to us or to him. This is an important part of stewardship, denial, and worship. Paul tells us in Romans 12:1 that we offer our "bodies" to God as our spiritual act of worship. Honor your body, and be kind to it by eating well.

Celebrate your victories when you have them. Throw parties, commemorate with a dinner, have a dance-off. Whatever works well within your community, do that.

Repeat this weekly. Go out of your way to find ways to do this and reasons to do these things. Can we be leaders in these areas, too?

4. Practice worship.

If you are an artist, you understand the importance of practice. Practice is that space where it is just you and your art together. In that space and time, you are trying to understand your art and make it become a part of who you are. Because of the demands of practicing, most of which is done alone, most of the work that you will do, musically, no one will ever see until they see you do it in public. Funny enough, when people see you perform your art in public—and if it is really good—they will never know the hours of practice and intention that you put into that art. However, if you tank in public, they know that you did not put in the work privately before you did it publicly. You can never hide that. You on a platform during worship can yield the same results both for better and for worse. Practice worshipping God. Whatever that looks like for you, do it. If you do not find your way to worship God privately, you cannot just turn it on once you get in front of a crowd. Public worship is an overflow of private practice.

Public worship is an overflow of private practice.

5. Get outside your comfort zone.

Multicultural ministry will not always feel comfortable. Many times, we cannot learn or grow without getting uncomfortable. For many of us, we will need to go out and actually look for ways to live outside of our comfort zone, particularly for those of us who live in the United States. Many places in our country are set up so that we can have it our way and stay comfortable. We have to go looking for it.

Look for opportunities to be in the minority somewhere. Have coffee with someone who has a different ethnic heritage than you in *that person's* neighborhood. Dance a little (for some of you that was way too far). Try something that you know you won't be good at. Visit a friend whose church's worship style is a little more or less expressive than your own. Whatever you do, just get out of your comfort zone and learn! You will not be sorry. (We will go deeper into this in chapter 8, so get ready!)

6. Be curious. Ask questions.

At some point in our adult lives, many of us stop being curious about life. We have enough figured out about the world around us and the people around us that we stop asking questions like "what's that?" or "why?" or "how?" Multicultural worship leaders are curious people. They poke at the things that have been and ask questions that may even challenge the things that they think they know. They seek to remain childlike in their approach to life and ministry and open to the multicultural world around them. There is much to learn when you are in a community of diverse people.

Be curious about culture. There is a unique opportunity within a multicultural church to discover and learn about culture. I have learned more about Korean, Hispanic/Latin, and Indian cultures than ever before, just by doing life with people who are different than me. Ask questions in safe relational environments. Ask *why* people do the things they do and not just *how* they do them. Learn the way different people think. Learn what different people value. Apply the new things that you learn into your worship services and your life as a worship leader.

Be curious about story. Because we are human, we all have a story—and a complex one at that. The more story we find out, the more story we can tell; and the more story we tell, the more we can continue to help frame what Jesus is doing in our church communities. Learn stories about culture and believe them. Listen to stories of racial profiling and racism. Listen to the stories of your White brothers and sisters who talk about fear of being called a racist. Listen to stories of people feeling like they have no seat at the table.

Then tell and make (you are creative for a reason) stories of redemption, joy, and celebration! Cry and laugh. Enjoy a good story!

Take Your Own Advice

My guess is that if someone who you lead in your ministry came to you and asked your advice about how to be a healthy leader in multicultural ministry that you may give him similar instruction. Maybe you should begin taking your own good advice and remembering that not only are you not a superhero, but also you are *quite* human and in need of many of the same things that you prescribe to others. Be kind to yourself and allow yourself to be loved by others, by yourself, and by the Lord and to learn from the diverse community around you. You are worth it, too.

Reflect

Where in your life might you have segregated or isolated yourself as a leader? What have you believed or even experienced that has led you to do this?

What is one creative habit you can begin to build into your schedule to feed your own creative soul? (Examples are songwriting thirty minutes each week, listening to your favorite music one hour each week, or going to see live music or art performed at least once in the next month or two.)

In what area do you need to get out of your comfort zone? How might you do that?

In what ways can you offer your "body" to God as a living sacrifice and spiritual act of worship? (Examples are intentional eating, more rest, and healthy thinking.)

Chapter 5
Know Yourself

Your story and your culture affect the way you perceive art, situations, and people. The first step toward relating to others is understanding yourself.

He Never Said a Mumblin' Word (a Parable)

Once upon a time there was a man who loved enunciation. Let's call him "the Enunciator." Every day he stood in front of a mirror and practiced saying words crisply and clearly. He taught his children tongue twisters at an early age and drilled them until they could say them perfectly. He corrected his wife when she slurred words or ran syllables together. He regularly (and usually politely) asked his coworkers not to mumble. He himself never said a mumblin' word.

After years of being a proponent of clear communication, the Enunciator started to recognize that all too often the people he talked to on the phone would mumble. He frequently had to ask people to repeat things. And he became frustrated with people's poor phone etiquette. And then there were fast-food restaurants with drive-thru windows. He didn't even try to understand *those* "mumbling fools." He would simply place his order, drive around, and hand the cashier a large enough bill to cover whatever the cost might be. Soon, he started to realize that the people in his office were letting their enunciation falter. More and more often he would have conversations with coworkers and only understand half of what they said. He asked them again and again not to mumble. They seemed oblivious to the issue. So, in an effort to be agreeable, he nodded his head often. And he would then ask his coworkers to write him memos about their conversations. He got some strange looks and some even stranger memos. He received memos about football scores from the day before and about how strong the coffee in the coffeepot was. He also received memos in which people assumed he had agreed to proposals he had never considered. "If people would only enunciate their words clearly, there would be no need for such ridiculousness," he thought.

It seemed that mumbling was reaching epidemic proportions. Even at home, he would often misunderstand his children because all their syllables were running together. He began to research speech therapy options for them. He became more and more frustrated with the people around him and everyone's failure to speak clearly. This fueled his own enunciation even more. He spoke so crisply and clearly that people around him thought he had some kind of disorder. One day when listening to the news anchorwoman mumble her way through a report on crime in his city, the Enunciator exploded. He screamed loudly but still clearly. "No more mumbling! I can't take it anymore! I am going to do something about this." He began to develop a website to help people with their enunciation. He recorded videos of his daily exercises and uploaded them to the website. He planned to launch a "No More Mumbling" campaign for local businesses and schools. He began to share the vision with anyone who would listen.

One day, the Enunciator was sharing his passion for enunciation along with a prototype of his website with a local businessman when the unthinkable happened. He was showing one of his enunciation exercise videos when he realized that he couldn't understand himself. Here he thought he had been speaking crisply and clearly, but as he watched himself on the video, it was obvious that he was mumbling. He could hardly make out every other word. His frustration soared to new levels. He quickly shut down the computer and apologized to the businessman for wasting his time. "I can't believe that I mumbled through that video. This is so embarrassing," he said. "What do you mean?" the businessman asked. "I think it was a great video! I could hear every syllable clearly and beautifully." The Enunciator didn't know what to say. He walked out of the meeting without so much as a crisp, clear good-bye.

Later that evening, through tears, the Enunciator shared with his wife what had happened at the business meeting earlier that day. She looked at him knowingly. "Have you ever thought of having your hearing checked?" she asked. The thought had never crossed his mind. But, obviously, it had crossed hers more than once. The next day, he visited the doctor and was quickly diagnosed with severe hearing loss. He began to understand that the problem was not so much with everyone else's enunciation, but with his perception. What he thought was reality was a misdiagnosis. What was once indistinct and frustrating became quite clear to him at last.

Crossing Cultures

In cross-cultural interaction, not only is it important for you to learn about other people and cultures and how they process and view things, but also it is of utmost importance that you *know yourself*. As you understand yourself, you will be able to discern better what assumptions you bring to cross-cultural interactions. Knowing these assumptions will enable you to fight against them and to intentionally seek other people's perspectives to help you. It is important to note:

Facial expressions do not mean the same thing to every culture.

Body language does not mean the same thing to every culture.

What is modest dress for one culture can be immodest dress in another culture.

Tone of voice does not mean the same thing to every culture.

Colors do not have the same connotations for every culture.

Physical interaction (touching one another) is not interpreted the same in every culture.

Starting a service too late for one culture could be starting too early for another culture.

Expectations of leaders are different in different cultures.

Music is not a universal language.

Let's double-click on that last statement for a minute. In 1835, Henry Wadsworth Longfellow made the statement that "music is the universal language of mankind" in his work entitled *Outre-Mer: A Pilgrimage Beyond the*

Sea ([New York: Harper and Brothers, 1835], 4). This has been quoted often, and many believe it to be true. But does music transcend culture? Music is definitely a universal phenomenon. It happens everywhere, in every nation of the world. But to say that it is a universal language implies that if you play notes of music here in the United States, people in the rain forest of Brazil will understand what those notes mean when they hear them. This is clearly not true. We each interpret music differently based on many factors, including experiences, culture, and personal taste.

Music is not a universal language.

Consider this true story about an American missionary woman living in the jungles of South America. One morning, she woke up feeling particularly joyful and began praising the Lord through song. Throughout the day, as she went about her tasks around her hut, she sang loudly the chorus of "How Great Thou Art." Later that day, the women of the village converged on her hut, and they were deeply concerned. "Why are you so sad today?" they asked. "Who died?" As it turns out, in this particular culture, long, sustained high notes are a characteristic of funeral music. They sing this way only when someone has died. So, as they heard the missionary sing "Then sings my soul . . . how great Thou art . . . how great Thou art!" they knew someone in her family must have died.[1] Why else would she sing long, high notes? They could not imagine those being used to praise God with gladness.

Recently, I (Josh) was illustrating the idea that music is not a universal language while training the teachers at our Proskuneo School of the Arts. It is important to note that our teachers are culturally diverse, representing a number of nations including Syria, the United States, Colombia, and Burma. I played some short melodies on the piano. The first I played was the motive from the song "Dueling Banjos." This was familiar to the Americans in the room, but the teachers from other countries had never heard it before. After playing the music, I asked them what kind of vehicle came to mind when they heard those notes. The Americans all responded that the song reminded them of a pickup truck. The non-American teachers were amazed. It didn't conjure images of any kind of vehicle for them. I then asked what items

---

1. Stuart K. Hine, "How Great Thou Art," Stuart K. Hine Trust, 1953.

might be in the back window of said pickup truck? The Americans responded in unison that they imagined a gun rack and a confederate flag based on those few notes of melody played. For some American teachers, these images conjured positive feelings, and for others, they conjured negative feelings. Nevertheless, all the Americans had the same associations. Next, I played the first few notes of the Colombian national anthem. I then asked how many of them had colors come to mind when they heard those notes. Only one teacher raised his hand. Everyone else looked shocked when the Colombian answered so decisively that the colors yellow, red, and blue came to mind. None of the rest of them had any images come to mind. They thought of things like "happiness," "thoughtfulness," and "longing" but no colors. Those music notes communicated different things to different people. This happens in our congregations every week. Music that touches my heart deeply does not affect my wife's heart in the least bit. And vice versa.

Heart Music

I have found the concept of "heart music" to be very helpful and clarifying. Some friends of mine have defined heart music as: "The musical system that most fully expresses his or her emotions. A person's heart music may include several different musical systems" (thanks to Brian Schrag and Paul Neeley). Your heart music moves you at a deeper level, sometimes bypassing your mind and going straight to your heart. It is the kind of music you listen to when no one else is around. My colleague Ian Collinge says that your heart music "feels like an old friend, evokes special memories, catches your breath, expresses the real you, and awakens your soul." I couldn't agree more.

Heart music "feels like an old friend, evokes special memories, catches your breath, expresses the real you, and awakens your soul."
—Ian Collinge

Our hearts are incredibly important to God. All throughout scripture we are encouraged and commanded that our hearts should be engaged in worshipping God. Consider a few of these.

The word of Christ must live in you richly. Teach and warn each other with all wisdom by singing psalms, hymns, and spiritual songs. Sing to God with gratitude *in your hearts*. (Col 3:16, emphasis added)

Praise the LORD!
I thank the LORD *with all my heart*
in the company of those who do right, in the congregation. (Ps 111:1, emphasis added)

Hypocrites! Isaiah really knew what he was talking about when he prophesied about you, *This people honors me with their lips, but their hearts are far away from me.* Their worship of me is empty since they teach instructions that are human rules. (Matt 15:7-9)

Because your heart is important to God, it is important for you to be aware of what your heart music is. Often our tendency is to believe that we are right and that others are wrong. Our heart music *feels* right to us. In fact, it is possible that the reason you believe a particular song is especially good for worship may be strongly tied to your own heart music and may not have much at all to do with the "quality" of the song. Have you ever considered this?

The reason you believe a particular song is especially good for worship may be strongly tied to your own heart music and may not have much at all to do with the "quality" of the song.

As a leader, once you are aware of your own heart music, there can be many benefits to your congregation. If you have walked through the process of discovering and understanding your own heart music, you can help your congregation members discover their heart music. As you become aware of how powerfully heart music can affect you personally, you can employ heart music carefully and intentionally to powerfully affect the diverse people whom you lead. As you are aware of how your heart music informs your own ideas of what is "good music" and what isn't, you can help your congregation members understand how their perspectives are shaped by their own heart music.

Reflect

What kind of music do you listen to when no one else is around?

What types of music have ever moved you so profoundly that they made you cry or dance?

Not in church, but privately:

> What kind of music helps you enter into a time of prayer?
>
> What kind of music helps you enter into a time of drawing close to God?
>
> What kind of music helps you enter into a time of praising God and exalting him?

(This is most likely your heart music!)

How does your own heart music affect the music that you choose to incorporate in worship services you plan and lead?

Are there certain musical styles that you think are inappropriate for worshipping God? Why?

Ethnocentrism

Going back to the parable of the Enunciator, we realize that, often our tendency is to think that we are right and others are wrong. This is ethnocentrism at its most basic level. The Enunciator assumed over and over again that the problem was with other people and not with himself. We do the same thing. For example, which side of the road is the correct side to drive on? Whichever side of the road we grew up driving on will *feel strongly* like the correct side. And as a result, the other side will *feel wrong* to us. Those feelings are completely normal and legitimate. And they inform our behavior. The challenge is that these things that have been ingrained in us by our culture and upbringing are often invisible to us. We are often completely unaware that we even have those feelings until we come in contact with someone who thinks or does things differently than we do. Take that driving example. You wouldn't know you have strong feelings about which side of the road to drive on until you go to another country where they do things differently. If you grew up in the United States, everyone knows that the right side of the road is the correct side for driving. It is unquestioned. And it is taken for granted. But, then one day, let's say you travel to Zimbabwe (or one of the other seventy-plus countries that drive on the left side of the road). You have to think about *everything*! You can't even cross the street without looking left, then right—oops, then left again. You go to the passenger side of your vehicle to get in before realizing the steering wheel is on the opposite side. The gear shift has to be maneuvered by your left hand, which feels completely awkward. Turning left or right requires significantly more thought and concentration than normal. And if there are no other cars on the road (from which you can take visual cues), you will probably be more likely to revert to what you are used to. Be careful! All the while, your feelings will tell you that everything about this is wrong. You may fight those feelings by telling yourself that when you are in Zimbabwe, you must do as the Zimbabweans do. But it is important to recognize your initial impulses and how they affect you. If you are unaware and leave your initial feelings and impulses unchecked, you will easily believe that the way Zimbabweans drive is wrong. Or at the very least it is inferior to the way you grew up driving. This is human nature. And you must be intentional to make yourself aware of it. This is why we are warned in Romans 12 not to think of ourselves more highly than we ought to think. Your way is not necessarily better, but it will necessarily *feel* better to you. And that is okay. What you do with that feeling is what matters.

Your way is not necessarily better, but it will necessarily *feel* better to you. And that is okay. What you do with that feeling is what matters.

Self-Awareness

It is of utmost importance that we know ourselves. Self-awareness could have spared the Enunciator (and those around him) a lot of heartache and trouble. If he had only known from the beginning of his own hearing loss, all of his frustration and damaged relationships could have been avoided. Self-awareness can be defined as having a clear perception of your personhood. This includes knowing your strengths and weaknesses, tendencies, ideals, beliefs, motivation, opinions, and emotions. Unless you understand yourself, you will not be able to understand other people and your interactions with them.

Sometimes, it can seem to us as Christians that self-awareness is a negative thing. It can seem more spiritual to avoid at all costs anything that has the word *self* in it. After all, we are to deny ourselves in order to follow Christ, right? Absolutely. But how can you deny yourself if you don't know yourself to begin with? How can you consciously give up something if you are unaware of it? Consider this scripture from Romans 12:3-8:

> Because of the grace that God gave me, I can say to each one of you: don't think of yourself more highly than you ought to think. Instead, be reasonable since God has measured out a portion of faith to each one of you. We have many parts in one body, but the parts don't all have the same function. In the same way, though there are many of us, we are one body in Christ, and individually we belong to each other. We have different gifts that are consistent with God's grace that has been given to us. If your gift is prophecy, you should prophesy in proportion to your faith. If your gift is service, devote yourself to serving. If your gift is teaching, devote yourself to teaching. If your gift is encouragement, devote yourself to encouraging. The one giving should do it with no strings attached. The leader should lead with passion. The one showing mercy should be cheerful.

Notice that we are encouraged to think about ourselves. We are warned not to think of ourselves too highly. And certainly, this is an issue. We will get to that in a minute. But we are exhorted in this passage to think about ourselves. And to do so with sober judgment and in light of God's grace. In the context of this passage, we realize that if we don't think of ourselves with sober judgment, we cannot function as we should in the body of Christ.

Part of thinking of ourselves with sober judgment is to understand the gifts that we have been given by God. We are to recognize the goodness and uniqueness of these gifts. If we don't, we can't use them as we should. If we don't know our gifts, we are not able to bring them to the table and leverage them for the good of others. Once we know what our gifts are, we are to use them wholeheartedly for the benefit of the body of Christ. But clearly, that all begins with thinking of ourselves rightly. Self-awareness is of great importance!

Reflect

What are your biggest strengths in leadership? Where would God have you use these most effectively? How would God have you use these most effectively?

What are your biggest weaknesses? How can you manage around these? How can you enlist others to help you in these areas?

Are you in the right place of service/leadership? Are you sure of God's call on your life to lead in this area?

Feedback

Another important thing we can learn from the Enunciator is that *we need other people's help and feedback in order to know ourselves well.* We need to process situations with other people (especially from different cultures) in order to have a better chance at understanding what is really happening. It wasn't until the Enunciator was able to share an experience with the businessman and hear himself speak that he had any indicator that maybe his perception was not reality. And it was his wife's suggestion to consider the possibility of hearing loss. Sometimes other people can know things about us (by observation, discernment, and so on) that we don't know about ourselves. There are people in your life who can give you really valuable feedback on who you are as a person. The question is, are you brave enough to ask them? And humble enough to listen and consider what they say?

Recently, a friend of mine (Josh) visited a Karen-Burmese church service. My friend speaks no Karen and didn't even try to make out the florid writing of the Karen script in the hymnal. He recognized a few of the tunes but was largely dependent on a translator (who gave him one sentence of translation every few minutes) so he could have some idea of what was going on. At one point, a young couple was brought to the front of the church. They were to be married the upcoming Saturday. They stood in front of the congregation looking ashamed (from my friend's perspective). Their heads were down and eyes were lowered. At one point, the pastor began to speak very intensely and passionately. About that time, the translator gave my friend one sentence to interpret this whole situation. He said, "The pastor says we must not have sex before marriage." In that moment, without realizing it, my friend let his own experiences, culture, and feelings inform his belief about what was happening in that moment. He took in the body language and facial expression of the couple as well as the passionate tone of the pastor, and he came up with his own interpretation. He assumed that this couple had been engaging in sexual relations before they were married and were now being brought in front of the church to have their sin exposed. He assumed that they were expressing shame by their body language and facial expressions.

Maybe that was the case. But that was not my first assumption when my friend told me about the situation. My first thought was that they were embarrassed to be standing in front of the congregation. For the most part, my Burmese friends do not like to be singled out or to be the center of attention. They find their comfort and identity as part of a group. Individuality is not a value for them like it is for most Americans. I immediately thought that the pastor simply took advantage of the upcoming wedding, which was present in most people's minds, to talk about sexual purity. I did not assume that his talk was in response to the couple's actions. My friend may have been right in his interpretation. I may be correct in my interpretation. (Of course, my human tendency is to think that I am right.) Or we both could be wrong and there is some other reality that we have yet to consider. My point is this. If my friend hadn't shared the experience and his interpretation with me, he would have gone on assuming that his interpretation was reality. He might not have even realized that he had interpreted the situation. He might have just assumed he knew what was going on. If we stay inside our own heads, our assumptions can become equated with reality. This is so dangerous!

Reflect

Oftentimes we ourselves are the common denominator in frustrating circumstances. Just like the Enunciator was the common denominator in each of those mumbling situations (work, home, phone, drive-thru, and news), you may be the common denominator in frustrating circumstances in different areas of your life. Pray through that. Ask the Lord for wisdom and discernment. Consider where your own feelings, assumptions, and interpretations might be at play.

DIALOGUE: Ask those closest to you (including a family member, a friend, a coworker, and someone you lead) to dialogue with you about your strengths and weaknesses. Pray beforehand that you are able to listen well, without defending yourself, and that God will help you to process rightly what you hear.

Chapter 6

Navigate Culture

Culture is always at work when there are people gathered for any reason. Take a look at some common cultural dynamics and how they relate to worship at your church.

I (Josh) have found that it is important for me as a multicultural worship leader to be a student of culture. I don't read books on sociology. But I do study and read about culture and the way it affects our behavior and perceptions. I do talk to the people I lead about their own cultural come-froms. After all, worship leading isn't just about leading music and worship. It is also about leading people.

I do not consider myself an expert on culture. But I have studied and thought at length about how our cultures affect our perspectives on life in general and corporate worship specifically. I hope this chapter might offer you a lightbulb moment or two. I hope it will inspire you to study more and have more conversations about these things. I hope that it will spur you on to become a student of culture as well.

I have chosen five cultural dynamics that may be at play at any given time on your worship team or in your congregation. My guess is that at one point or another you have dealt with each of these cultural phenomena without even realizing it.

Time—Event

Probably one of the most obvious differences people recognize between cultures is the way they interact with time. Even in mono-ethnic churches, there are people with different cultural approaches to time. Some people think they are late if they are not five minutes early. Others have never been early for anything in their life. Some leave at noon whether the service is over or not. Others only leave when the lights in the sanctuary are turned off on them. Most often it is not the ones who arrive late who leave right at noon. I have heard Koreans talk about "Korean-time" and Dominicans talk about "Dominican-time."

I have heard many people say things like, "Well, some people are time oriented, and some just aren't." I cringe when I hear things like that. Why? Because it reveals a bias. People who talk this way leave no room in their language for someone to be oriented around anything other than time. They are either time oriented or not. I prefer to say that most people are either "time oriented" or "event oriented."

Our American culture, in general, is very time oriented. I have said things to my children like, "Be ready to go at 12:13." I have had the urge to text employees when they were two minutes late. These are both strong indicators of time orientation. Time-oriented people value punctuality and are more prone to set limits and goals. Many American churches are very time oriented. I have seen service order charts that have each element timed, and sometimes down to the seconds. I have often led in churches in which there is a large clock counting down the milliseconds so that the worship leader is always keenly aware of how much time is elapsing. I have been told in some churches that when the clock reaches 00.00, I must be walking off the stage. These are all strong indicators of time orientation. Though our American culture is very time oriented, it is important to realize that there are always people within a given culture who do not conform to cultural norms. So, there are likely Americans (and non-Americans) in your church who are more event oriented than time oriented.

Time-oriented people value punctuality and are more prone to set limits and goals.

Event-oriented cultures and people think of their daily schedule as moving from one event to another. Their schedule might be: finish work, eat dinner, go to worship rehearsal, go to bed. They don't necessarily assign specific times to each of these. They just do them until they are done. And then they move on to the next thing. They are more concerned with the details of the event rather than the timing of it. People who are more event oriented often have a come-what-may attitude and are more focused on the present. In event-orientation cultures, the service starts when everyone who needs to be there is present. It starts when everything that needs to be in place is set. It starts when it starts. And it ends when it is finished. Most of the congregations my family and I visit in our community are more event oriented. And their services last anywhere from two to three and a half hours. Recently, my family attended a mostly White American church. We were in and out of the sanctuary in under one hour. When the benediction was pronounced, my kids looked at me in amazement and said, "Is it over?" They couldn't believe it.

Event-oriented cultures and people think of their daily schedule as moving from one *event* to another.

Helpful Hints

- Whenever possible, it is wise not to schedule every minute of a worship rehearsal. It is wise to leave some time for relating to one another and for people arriving late. If I know we need about one hour of rehearsing time, I will usually schedule a one-hour-and-thirty-minute rehearsal.

- When you are planning for a worship service, have a plan, but do not schedule every minute. This allows your time-oriented people to work the plan. (If you are a completely event-oriented worship ministry, you very well may lose the time-oriented people.) This allows your event-oriented people to feel a little more at ease and also allows for spontaneity, which can be a blessing for everyone involved. If you have twenty minutes of musical worship allotted, don't plan to sing five different songs in those twenty minutes. In a multicultural community especially, it is important to build in a margin.

- If starting on time is an important value for your context, communicate about this clearly, and give extra practical help to those who might not be prone to punctuality. If you frequently do not start on time, have something for the punctual people to do when they arrive so they don't waste their time.

- If you are often schedule-/goal-oriented in your ministry, it may be helpful to schedule some time for people simply to hang out with one another. This could be the perfect time for some of your event-oriented people to take the lead.

- Be careful with your language. If you are frustrated that a particular culture tends to arrive late for church, be careful what you say about them. And take note that they are probably some of the best relationship builders and lingerers you have. Help others who are frustrated realize that there are positives and negatives to both time orientation and event orientation.

Relationships—Task

I feel this tension inside me all the time. The Dominican in me is quite content to (and really desires to) just sit with people and enjoy their company. I want to know everything that is going on in your life. I want to listen and laugh and linger. But the White American inside me is very concerned with getting the job done. I love to cross things off my task list. (In fact, sometimes I write things on the list that I have already done, just so I can cross them off.) Sometimes, in order to get things done, I have to cut conversations short or say no to people's requests to just hang out. Other times, in order to connect with people and build meaningful relationships, I need to put my phone away or set my task list aside.

Relationship-oriented people find satisfaction in interaction with others. Their relationships are long-term and committed.

Most people and cultures tend toward either task or relationship. This is not to say that they don't value the other. It is to say that when there is a choice between the two, they will choose one of them consistently more often. I can watch one worship rehearsal and tell fairly easily whether a worship team is more task oriented or relationship oriented. Some worship rehearsals I have been to are all business. People rehearse on their own ahead of time and then when they come together, they cut to the chase, ask important questions, nail things down and then they are finished. Worship rehearsal can take forty-five minutes or less in these settings, and many times the team members don't know one another at all. Some worship rehearsals I have been to are all about relationship. The band members spend the first while catching up with each other. Whenever the worship leader stops a song for some reason, people immediately carry on side conversations with one another. There is time for prayer and studying God's word together. There are more questions about each other's lives than about the service they are preparing for. They know each other very well, and often they show up for Sunday's service unprepared. Task-oriented people on a relational team will likely be completely frustrated. And relationship-oriented people on a task-oriented team will likely feel disconnected and lonely.

Relationship-oriented people find satisfaction in interaction with others. Their relationships are long-term and committed. Task-oriented people find satisfaction in achieving their goals. When the reason for a relationship changes, it is fine (from their perspective) for the relationship to change. Relationship-oriented people don't understand this at all. For example, if someone were to step off the worship team for a season, a task-oriented person would be okay not seeing or talking with that person. After all, he or she isn't part of the team anymore. But a relationship-oriented person will still go out of her way to connect with her friend even though they are not still on the team together. (If a relational person leaves the team for some reason, it can be hurtful if no one from the team pursues friendship with her!)

Task-oriented people find satisfaction in achieving their goals. When the reason for a relationship changes, it is fine (from their perspective) for the relationship to change.

Helpful Hints

- Build time in your rehearsals for relating to one another.
  Spending time talking with one another, reading the Bible

together, and praying for one another build your team. It will be especially meaningful for the relational people in your group. And if you make it part of the practice schedule, the task-oriented people will see it as something important to check off their lists.

- Find ways to relate to people outside of services and rehearsals. This may also be a good time to invite former worship team members to hang out with everyone.

- If you are a relationship-oriented person, try making a task list (a short one might be good to start) and sticking to it. If you are a task-oriented person, try putting your task list away for an afternoon and go have a cup of coffee with someone you minister alongside. Linger longer than you feel like you should.

Power Distance

Some of you may even balk at that heading. If so, you are likely low power distance. You will see what I mean in a minute. A friend of mine has said that power is not a bad thing. The important thing is how it is used. I couldn't agree more. People and cultures tend to be either high power distance or low power distance. In high-power-distance cultures, the leader is separate from the people and more authoritarian. Obedience is important, and followers are given little to no input into decisions. In low-power-distance cultures (like the United States), the power is controlled by the people, and the process is extremely participatory. There is a lot of discussion, and people are seen as independent.

In high-power-distance cultures, the leader is separate from the people and more authoritarian. Obedience is important, and followers are given little to no input into decisions.

Traditionally, churches in the United States were higher power distance. The separation of the people and the platform creates a distance. The pulpit is a barrier (visible separation) of sorts between the people and the pastor. In some denominations, the pastor has almost complete authority in the church.

It would be disrespectful to question his judgment or decisions. This is high power distance. In other denominations, the people can vote the pastor out of office. They have no problem telling the pastor what he should do differently. This is low power distance. Lately, it seems, many churches in the United States, regardless of denominations, have begun having their pastor preach in a more conversational way, sometimes even sitting down on the level of the people. This is an expression of low power distance. The idea of Jesus as King is a high-power-distance concept, while the idea of Jesus as Shepherd is a low power distance. And clearly, and thankfully, Jesus is both.

In low-power-distance cultures, the power is controlled by the people, and the process is extremely participatory. There is a lot of discussion, and people are seen as independent.

In high-power-distance congregations, there is often a lot of respect and verbal honor shown to leaders. In low-power-distance congregations, the leader tries to be seen as one of the congregation. In high-power-distance congregations, often the front/platform/stage is a place of power. Only certain people are allowed to go up front. Only certain people are allowed to sit in those large chairs on the stage. In low-power-distance congregations, there is no platform or stage. Anyone can go or sit anywhere.

Helpful Hints

- Consider how you are using the power you have been given. Who might God have you share your power with?

- If you are a leader in your context, how do you want the people who follow you to perceive you? Do you want to come across like you are one of them? Or do you want them to respect you and honor your position of leadership? Or maybe both?

- Are the people who lead you high or low power distance? How do you think this should affect the way you interact with them?

Context

Are the setting and process in which an event takes place important? Is the format important or just the content? These are questions of context. In general, cultures tend to be either high context or low context.

High-context cultures, on the one hand, believe that the setting, location, and process of an event are as important as the event itself. Recently, I organized the entertainment for a festival in our community. I was not in charge of assigning different performers to venues, but I was responsible for making sure that everything went smoothly. In the middle of the day, I was approached by the Ethiopian manager of an Ethiopian dancer who was to perform in the gym. He was irate. He told me, in no uncertain terms, that the gym was not an appropriate place for her dance performance. "There are people playing basketball in there!" he exclaimed. Because I had studied this cultural concept of context, I immediately knew what he was saying. Assigning the dancer to the gym communicated to him that she was not as important as those who were assigned to the auditorium. (Though, for the organizers, who were American, the assignments were made based on audio capabilities and other functional issues.) For him, something beautiful and expressive should not and could not happen in an environment like a gym. He was insulted. We made some adjustments and allowed her to perform on the stage in the auditorium. And though there were very few people in the audience, he was satisfied because the context matched the content. High-context cultures tend to pay more attention to body language, facial expression, and tone of voice and not simply to what is being said. *How* is as important as *what*.

High-context cultures believe that the setting, location, and process of an event are as important as the event itself. High-context cultures tend to pay more attention to body language, facial expression, and tone of voice and not simply to what is being said. *How* is as important as *what*.

Low-context cultures, on the other hand believe that the content is more important than the setting. They tend to be more analytical in their thinking and can separate content from context. For them, a magazine on the topic of multicultural worship that is written by people from all one culture is fine, as long as the content is good. Because the Americans planning the festival I mentioned above were low context, they thought nothing of putting a traditional cultural dance in the gym. It had the most appropriate sound system for such a performance. It did not occur to them that the smell of sweaty basketball players might not be conducive to setting the scene for the beautiful dancing. They were thinking analytically. Low-context people don't see the need to dress up for special occasions. After all, what makes those occasions special (from their perspective) is the reason for the occasion. Certain church cultures value dressing up more highly than others. These cultural values are not wrong or right (both types of churches can come up with biblical reasons why they should dress up or dress down), but it is helpful to be aware what they might communicate to someone else. Sometimes, low-context people think that high-context people are too concerned with outward appearances. Low-context people might quote the scripture, "Have no regard for his appearance or stature, because I haven't selected him. God doesn't look at things like humans do. Humans see only what is visible to the eyes, but the LORD sees into the heart" (1 Sam 16:7). However, high-context cultures might reply that clearly clothing for worship is important to God based on Revelation 7:9-12.

Low-context cultures believe that the content is more important than the setting. They tend to be more analytical in their thinking and can separate content from context. Low-context people don't see the need to dress up for special occasions.

It is important to note, as we look at this cultural tension (and, in fact, *all* the tensions we consider in this chapter), that God is indeed both high context and low context. He came to a manger (low context) and will one day come riding a white horse (high context). Isaiah 57:15 says, "I live on high, in holiness, and also with the crushed and the lowly, reviving the spirit of the lowly, reviving the heart of those who have been crushed."

Helpful Hints

- Consider the space where worship happens with your congregation. Is it high or low context? How does this affect the people?

- Find ways to value both high- and low-context people for what they bring to the team/congregation. When it is time to decorate something, consider asking the high-context people. When it is time to find a worship leader for a camping trip, choose a low-context person.

- Consider what messages you are sending with the way you dress. Do people find you unapproachable? Or disrespectful? Consider ways you can promote understanding.

Direct and Indirect Communication

Some aspects of culture are connected. For example, indirect communication is most often connected with high-context culture. And direct communication connects with low-context culture. This makes sense because in high-context cultures, you may use words, but your body language or tone of voice may convey the true message. And high-context people pick up on that. In low-context cultures, the surroundings are not contributing to the message, so the words must be clear and direct.

Indirect communicators understand the messages that are being conveyed even if the words don't clearly state them.

In the South of the United States, White Americans are famous for indirect communication. Rather than saying, "I don't like green beans," we teach our kids to say, "Green beans are not my favorite." If I think your hat looks hideous, I might say, "My! What a statement that hat makes!" Direct communicators tend to believe that this kind of indirect communication is deceitful. While indirect communicators understand the messages that are being conveyed even if the words don't clearly state them. Let me give you an example. The other morning, we heard a knock on our door, and our neighbor (let's call her Miss Mable) was there to greet us. She took a whiff and said, "Something smells good in there." To which I replied that it must be the coffee that I was holding. Nothing beats the fragrance of coffee. Miss Mable looked straight at me, smiled, and said, "Gimme some of that!" pointing to my coffee. I have to admit I was caught off guard for a minute. My form of communication in that scenario would be much more indirect. If I was standing at my neighbor's door and wanted some coffee, I might say something like, "Mmm. Warm coffee sure would feel good on a chilly morning like this one." To which the neighbor (if well versed in indirect communication) would say, "Absolutely! Would you like to come in and have some?" I would smile and say, "Don't mind if I do." (Actually, I wouldn't say that last phrase, as it sounds like something from a generation or two ago, but you get the idea.) Instead of the pleasantries, Miss Mable cut straight to the chase. "Gimme some of that!" Direct communicators say exactly what they mean without mincing words. Often, indirect communicators take a longer way around.

Direct communicators say exactly what they mean without mincing words.

Sometimes, indirect communicators will decline something they wish to accept. For example, when I am offering a gift to someone, he will gently decline the gift to be polite. This can even carry over to offering someone a place on the worship team or a slot in a performance of some kind. Sometimes, when I offer my Asian friends an opportunity to perform (share their gifts with others), they will decline in order to show humility and to make sure that you really want them to participate. If you really want them to participate, you should know to ask again and again. When I was traveling with some Korean musician friends in Seoul, South Korea, I asked them, "How many times do I need to offer you to do something so that you know that I am really serious?" They said three was the magic number for them. You can see how this may come into play when you are interacting with indirect communicators. If you suspect someone is an indirect communicator, don't take what he says at face value. At least consider how he said it. Oftentimes, indirect communicators will do what they can to avoid saying no. They want to avoid making either of you look bad in any way. So, you might ask someone if she could play a violin solo on a certain jazz piece you want to do in church next Sunday. You heard through the grapevine that she is a great violin player, and you think a violin would be perfect for this song. What you don't know is that she is a classically trained musician who is only comfortable reading notes and not playing improvisationally. She doesn't want you to look bad for not knowing her well enough to make an appropriate request of her. She also may not want to admit her own inability. Rather than say no and tell you why she can't do it, she might say, "I will think about it," or, "Maybe some other time." If you take her literally, you may come back to ask her if she thought about it. Not a great idea. She clearly communicated no to you in an indirect way. But if you are a direct communicator, you could have missed it. So, what can you do in this situation? Consider asking her what kind of music she enjoys playing on the violin. If she tells you that she enjoys classical music, you can ask, "What do you think about jazz music?" If she says, "I like to listen to it, but I have not played it very much," you have your answer. And now you can look for a creative way to incorporate a classical violin piece in a worship service in the near future.

Helpful Hints

- It is not helpful to ask indirect communicators questions that can be answered with a simple yes or no. Learn to ask open-ended questions and not put people on the spot.

- Look at who you have on your worship team or in your ministry. Are they mostly direct communicators? Perhaps you haven't asked the indirect communicators enough so they know you really want them to be involved. A direct communicator (like Miss Mable) will likely come straight up to you and tell you that she'd like to be involved.

- If you are an indirect communicator, please understand that a direct communicator may not understand when you are saying no. If you believe someone is a direct communicator, a gentle no could be very helpful for him. As far as he is concerned, you can say no and still be polite.

- If you are an indirect communicator, resist the urge to think that direct communicators are simply being rude. And if you are a direct communicator, resist the urge to think that indirect communicators are being deceitful.

If you are serving in a culturally diverse ministry, these five tensions that we have explored briefly in this chapter will likely come up often. First, it is important that you be aware so that you can fight against your natural reaction in those circumstances. Second, it can be helpful for you to consider how you might change your interactions with people based on their cultural come-from. Last, it could be extremely helpful for you to find gentle ways to help the different cultures you interact with to understand one another. Even reading one of these sections during a team meeting or a worship rehearsal could be the starting point to a good discussion and more understanding among your team. No matter how much you have studied these things, please know that every culture has people who function along the cultural norms and others who defy them. Get to know the people God has surrounded you with. Don't approach these conversations as an expert, but as a fellow learner. And may you be an agent of God's peace.

Chapter 7
Culture Coaches

What is a culture coach? Why should you have one?
Why should you be one?

Although researching a culture or language on the Internet can be helpful, it is at best an incomplete approach. There are people who have done online research and then considered themselves an expert on a particular culture or nation. They have never even talked to someone from that nation. The point is not simply to learn information. The end goal is to learn how to live in God-honoring community with people who are different from you. The best way to do this is by developing real, honest relationships. This takes time. But it is extremely valuable. In the end, you want the people in your congregation to do more than simply sit in the same pew with one another and sing one another's songs. You want them to know one another, love one another, and share with one another. As a leader, you need to pursue multicultural relationships (remember chapters 3 and 4).

You could simply go on YouTube and learn a worship song in Yoruba (Nigerian language). You might be able to get the pronunciation pretty close just by listening. You could memorize the song, lead it on Sunday, and feel like a success. But what if you were to get to know someone in your congregation who is from Nigeria? Imagine this scenario. You invite him to your house for a meal and ask him to bring recordings of some of his favorite songs in Yoruba. From his list of favorites, you pick a song that seems easy to learn. You ask him to tell you why he likes that particular song and to help you understand what it means in English. You take a few weeks to practice the song on your own. You listen to it on your way to work. You practice singing it and write out a phonetic guide that makes sense to you. Then you get together with your friend again and sing it for him. He corrects your pronunciation in a few places. He helps you figure out how to make the sounds that are more difficult for you. You laugh together about how silly it sounds when you are trying to pronounce certain syllables. When your friend says you are ready, you teach the song to your worship team (you have sent them a recording ahead of time). You invite your friend to rehearsal and ask him to tell the team why he likes this song. Then you ask him to teach the team the pronunciation of the words in Yoruba. You share your own feelings of insecurity and difficulties learning the song with your team. They learn the song, and now you are ready to introduce it to the congregation. You invite your Nigerian friend to introduce the song in the worship service. He tells a little about the song and why it is meaningful to him, explains the language, and teaches a word or phrase in Yoruba to the congregation (see chapter 14).

In the first scenario (in which you learn the song on your own by searching YouTube), you sing a song in Yoruba in church. In the second scenario, you also sing a song in Yoruba in church. But in the second scenario, because you take the time to get to know someone and learn from him, the results are much broader, richer, and more enduring. In the second scenario, you are building a friendship. You are connecting with your new friend on various occasions over the period of weeks or even months. You are connecting your new friend with other friends of yours. You are offering your friend the opportunity to lead the entire church, if even for a moment or two. You are sure that the song you are singing actually connects to the heart of at least one of the Nigerians in your congregation. You are connecting with your worship team at a more vulnerable level. And you have someone you can ask questions to when you have more questions about the Yoruba language or Nigerian culture. Later, you could ask what parts of the worship service he really connects with or what parts of the service seem foreign to him. You could ask him what is one thing he would change about the worship service at your church if he could. The possibilities for stretching, learning, and growing are great.

If you desire to learn more about a specific culture, we strongly encourage you to look for someone to be a culture coach for you. Look for someone inside that culture who would allow you to ask honest (sometimes blunt) questions to help you understand. If possible, look for someone who has a good understanding of his own culture as well as your culture. He can help you process some of the differences and potential points of conflict. There are many things you can learn from this person that you could never learn from the Internet or a book. In relationship, we learn nuances. We learn to look beyond stereotypes to individuals and how they are affected by and relate to their culture. In relationship, we can process together our fears and insecurities. We can press in to the Lord together and let him teach us through each other. In relationship, we are given the wonderful gift of getting outside ourselves.

What Is a Coach?

In this season in my (Nikki's) life as an artist and a leader, one of my favorite roles is that of coach. I am a vocal coach. I am a coach for worship leaders and for those who are just beginning to lead ministries within their churches. My role as a coach has so many layers to it. I listen. I learn. I lead. I pass on what I have learned over the years. I help vocalists get from where they are to where they want to go in the next stage of their singing. I show worship leaders how to acquire the skills to get better and improve beyond their current abilities. Everyone who comes to me for coaching is looking to move beyond where they are and what they currently know to a fuller, more knowledgeable, more effective version of themselves as artists or creative people. When we want to get better, we find a coach. When you want to be more effective and knowledgeable in the area of *multicultural* worship, ministry, and relationship, you should find a culture coach.

Add Value to Life

Not too long ago, I received a call from my sweet friend Heidi. Heidi had just moved into a new neighborhood to intentionally minister to and serve the people there with the love of Jesus. Heidi is probably one of only a handful of White people who still live in this particular neighborhood that now is home to an array of different cultures from all around the world. One of the first things that Heidi did when she arrived was to visit the large African American church in town and begin to build relationships. Heidi quickly began to be keenly aware of so many cultural differences between her and her new friends, hence the phone call to me. "Will you be my culture coach?" she said. It was actually the first time that I had ever heard that term and the first time that I had been asked quite like that. My response? "Of course!" Heidi then began to tell me how she wanted to know if I would just be available to her when she had questions about African American culture. She wanted to

81

hear my perspective on the world and on situations that happen around us in our country. She wanted to be able to ask me questions about how I do my hair and why something in the news might make me angrier than it makes her. She wanted to know about customs in my culture and why certain things were the way that they were even in church culture. She wanted to learn about my experience through my words and my informal teaching.

If you are a part of the dominant culture group in any country or even within a church, you could go most of your life without engaging with the nondominant community or learning its language or customs. It is easy for you to survive and thrive without engaging.

Choosing a culture coach adds value to the person you are asking. It is an invitation to be known. It is an invitation into relationship. It is an invitation to pass on what someone has learned. It is a beautiful thing when you ask someone to teach you what she has learned so that your life can be enriched, culturally. It adds value to who she is as a person and gives even more dignity and value to her own cultural experience. If in the community or country that you live in, you are part of the dominant culture, this is even more powerful. Why? Because you don't "have to." Engaging in any activity because you "want to" speaks. When you are part of the dominant culture and you make a decision to share your life and your experience with nondominant cultures around you, it adds value. The reality is that if you are a part of the dominant culture group in any country or even within a church, you could go most of your life without engaging with the nondominant community or learning its language or customs. It is easy for you to survive and thrive without engaging. It speaks volumes when you choose to learn from people of other cultures who are not used to being asked to share their experiences and when you listen to their lives.

Conversely, when you are the nondominant culture and you extend grace to people in the dominant culture group, you are showing and speaking a level of humility and grace that is not culturally normal. Why? Because you don't "have to" either. When you live and exist within nondominant cultural spheres, you are used to people in the dominant culture not needing you. You can also find yourself accustomed to holding onto your pain (and for good reason) and sometimes even directing your pain at a dominant culture that you believe does not understand you. So, why would you extend yourself and help them?

> When you are the nondominant culture and you extend grace to people in the dominant culture group, you are showing and speaking a level of humility and grace that is not culturally normal.

What if a multicultural community of Jesus-followers would rise up together and educate one another by sharing their experiences even in the face of their own cultural pain? What if instead of slapping each other on the wrist every time we made a cultural mistake, we press through our pain and educate through coaching instead of arguing?

I cannot appropriately express to you the delight I feel as a coach of artists when I see them succeeding and putting into practice the experiences that I poured into them. It is as fulfilling to me as it is to them. Finding someone who is willing to be a culture coach is a worthwhile investment that adds value to our lives and to the lives of those coaching us.

Have Backup When You Mess Up

I am not sure that anybody would actually want to say this out loud, but I'm going to do it. Everybody needs backup. If you find yourself in a situation where you've put your foot in your mouth with your words about culture, you are going to need it, too. I remember a time here in the United States when a famous radio personality got into some hot water with listeners because he made some disparaging statements about a women's basketball team, their skin color, and the way that they chose to wear their hair. As soon as the statements were made, people were calling for his firing, and they had already called in the "big guns" (that is, Al Sharpton and Jesse Jackson). People were calling him a racist and calling for his immediate firing. My question? Where were all of this guy's African American friends? Why weren't they coming to his aide and his defense? Where were his close Black friends who were vouching for his character? There was nothing but silence. I am using an extreme example to make this point that we are all going to put our foot in our mouth, so to speak, at some point in this journey toward God's multicultural church. Hopefully, we will not have been intentionally offensive. But in our quest to grow, change, and learn as a leader of diverse peoples, we will certainly make mistakes both privately and publicly. Wouldn't it be good to have someone come alongside us and vouch for our character if we happen to make a bad mistake?

Hopefully, your culture coach is a friend of yours already. If not, the hope is that the relationship will be friendly and this person will actually get an idea of who you are as a person by spending time with you and sharing wisdom and knowledge about her culture. Your culture coach is one of the first people you should expect to come running to your side when you find yourself in an awkward cultural situation. Having a great culture coach can also keep you from finding yourself in too many of those situations because she will alert you ahead of time to any cultural land mines that you might unknowingly be about to step on.

Check Your Blind Spot

Oftentimes when I (Nikki) drive I am surprised by bikers on the road. You'd think by now that there are enough people on bikes pedaling around that I would be used to seeing them, but I confess that I am not quite there yet in my "biker awareness." I don't know many bikers, and I don't have any in my family. In fact, I don't even own a bike. So they tend to surprise me when they show up in my blind spot. Sometimes someone just needs to mention it to me in a nonharsh way, in a "hey, there is a biker to your left" sort of way. Kind, considerate, and looking out for me. We can't always see what's in our blind spot (hence the term), and even though not intentional, our lack of awareness to what is in it can have damaging consequences. Having culture coaches to check your ministry blind spots is key. People who are speaking into your life, culturally, can also see areas within your ministry context where you may be unintentionally keeping people out or discouraging them from being involved in the ministry. It is critical to have people around you who will love you enough to point out potential for cultural misunderstandings and consequences within your ministry context.

Challenge Ministry Structures

Right now you may be wondering why you cannot find more volunteers to serve in your ministry. You've done everything that you know how to do to invite people into your ministry space and be a part of this glorious work that your church has been called to. Culture coaches can ask good questions regarding your ministry structures and oftentimes can expose unintentional hindrances to different cultures wanting to be a part of what you do. For instance, let's say that your multicultural church is made up of mostly Korean people and Indian people worshipping together. Maybe 90 percent of your choir is currently Korean and you are wondering why more of the Indian people within your church are not contacting you to be a part of the ministry. Having an Indian culture coach could be a helpful asset to your ministry life. What a lovely gift to be able to contact that person and ask him to take a look at what you do and tell you if there could be anything, culturally speaking, that may be hindering the Indian cultures in your church from participating. Culture coaches can look through their own cultural lenses and see things that you would never be able to see because you are not from that particular culture. The wisdom you gain from your cultural coach could give you valuable insight into cultural nuances and completely transform the way that you structure you ministry and increase your overall diversity.

Culture coaches can look through their own cultural lenses and see things that you would never be able to see.

How to Find a Culture Coach

- Find someone who you are already in relationship with, someone you trust.

- Get out there and *ask*! Most of us are way too scared that we will look like an idiot to just humble ourselves and ask.

- Be clear about what it is you need and why you need it. This will help both you and your potential coach be clear on the motive and will help people not feel like "tokens."

- Look for people who are bridge-builders, that is, people you know who are open to sharing their cultural experiences.

- Persevere if someone tells you no. Keep looking. Someone will say yes.

You, the Culture Coach

Not only should you find a culture coach if you need one, but also you may want to consider becoming one as well. When it comes to understanding the culture of another, many of us can feel like first-graders in our knowledge. The truth is, however, that when it comes to sharing our own cultural experiences, we are at the college-graduate level. Therefore, we are an expert in something—our own experience. When you become a culture coach for someone else, you open up the floodgates of honest living and being in touch with who you have been and are becoming as a person of color. Yes, that's what I said: we are all people of color. The greatest thing about becoming a culture coach is that you don't need certification or a degree from any university. All you need to do is share your life and your experience.

Benefits of Becoming a Culture Coach

First, becoming a culture coach allows you to embrace that you have a culture, too, and it is important and worthy of being shared. It is so empowering when you can intentionally share elements of your culture with someone who might otherwise not be able to experience it. If you are a White person, when is the last time that you had Black people over to your house for green bean casserole and ambrosia salad? Is that what it's called? You do know that many of us Black people say that those things are "White food"? See, I just taught you something. If you are a Black person, when was the last time that you invited White people over to your house for collard greens, baked macaroni and cheese, and red Kool-Aid? Did you know that some people say that's "Black food"? I know I am making sweeping generalizations about culture, and I hope you know that my intention is to get you to laugh a little; but my point is very serious. Becoming a culture coach can allow all of us to embrace our own culture and hold it in high regard as something valuable to be passed on to our multicultural friends.

Second, becoming a culture coach allows you to rejoice and not curse the cultural experiences you've had, and it allows God to use that part of your story, too. We all have elements of our cultural stories and ancestry that we would rather forget. However, they are what they are. And becoming a culture coach can help you learn how to embrace your histories as just that— yours. Sharing our cultural stories and how we process them can be truly empowering for so many of us who feel ashamed of our cultural background. Being able to share, teach, and coach others is a beautiful way to affirm the journey that we have been on as peoples of color.

So, in closing, who needs a culture coach? You do. Who should become a culture coach? You should.

Reflect

Is there a specific culture that you wish to learn more about? Who could you ask to be your culture coach for that culture?

How can you find ways to share your culture and come-from with others to promote understanding?

Section III

Hamstrings, *American Idol*, and Didgeridoos

[Leading change for the greater good]

Chapter 8

Stretch Yourself

The calling of a multiethnic worship leader, among other things, is the call to be a lifelong learner. Before you can stretch others, you must be willing to stretch yourself.

I Don't Speak Amharic

I (Josh) was the only person with white skin on the premises. In fact, I was the only non-Ethiopian at the Ethiopian Orthodox church in my community that Sunday. I walked in the door and was greeted in Amharic. I don't speak Amharic. I didn't even understand the greeting. The extent of my Amharic is one song that I learned from a friend and the ever-important phrase, "Thank you." The people who greeted me were smiling and seemed friendly enough, so I just smiled and nodded. (This is dangerous at times, but it felt like the right thing to do in this moment. My options were definitely limited.) I made my way into the crowded foyer where only women and small children lingered, and there I saw a large pile of shoes. I surmised that I was to take off my shoes, which I did, and leave them in the pile. Immediately I was grateful that the holes in my socks were not big enough to be noticed. I pushed through the door and entered the sanctuary. At first, it was both difficult to see and difficult to breathe. The incense in the room was so thick. I noticed that the men were sitting on the left side of the room and the women were on the right. I have been in many churches in my community that have men and women seated separately. And I have sat on the wrong side before because I was not paying attention. I finally know to look for this, and so I chose to sit on the left side with the other men.

91

There was a thick red and gold curtain across the front of the room, and soon some of the leaders emerged from behind it. Throughout the service those who were officiating went in and out of the curtain, and I couldn't help but wonder what was back there. I imagined it was a bit like the holy of holies and was clearly reserved for only a few. I knew that I was not part of that few. We began to sing songs of praise in Amharic. The words were projected on a screen, but I do not read the Amharic script. I stared at the screen and tried to make sense of the squiggles and dots for a few minutes but eventually gave up. I resorted to what I often do in churches where I don't understand the language. I settled for clapping along with the songs and stopped trying to sing. But quickly, I realized that I was not able to match everyone else's clapping pattern. I watched and tried to imitate for a while, still to no avail. At that point, a frustration rose up inside me. I have a degree in music. I consider myself to have pretty good rhythm. I love to analyze and learn non-Western musical styles. And I couldn't even clap along? I sat down, took out my journal, and began charting the claps and the rests. It certainly wasn't a typical American 4/4 pattern. But, once I charted it, I could at least clap along.

The service was long, and I understood only a few words, most of which were English words appropriated into Amharic such as *credit card* and *traffic*. I took in the ornate decorations, the white head coverings of the women, and the mostly European art that adorned the walls. At one point a boy emerged from behind the curtain holding a beautifully decorated umbrella over a Bible. At the end of the service, everyone (including me) formed a line and moved toward the front of the church. At the front of the line was a cross, toward which everyone took their turn to bow and kiss. I was in the line before I realized what it was all about. As I was standing there, it hit me that I was soon going to have my own turn to bow and kiss toward the cross. It was in that moment that a beautiful thought occurred to me. The name of the organization I lead is Proskuneo. It is a Greek word commonly translated as *worship* but literally means "to bow and kiss toward." I took my turn, and as I did, I said in my heart, "Jesus, I need you. I worship you." It was the first time I ever "proskuneo-ed" in church. I haven't been that far outside my comfort zone in a long time.

Comfort Zones

My family (my wife, Jennifer, and four children) and I worship in a different congregation here in our community every week. We have worshipped at Nepali, Liberian, Ethiopian, Hispanic, African American, Indian, Burundi, Congolese, Sudanese, Korean, Nigerian, Burmese, and many multicultural services all in the last year. We are comfortable reading an order of worship to know exactly what will happen next. And we are accustomed to having no idea what is happening even as it is taking place. We are used to taking visual cues about when to sit or stand because we don't understand the words that are being sung and preached. It is normal for us to be the only White Americans in the sanctuary. We attend some services that are finished in one hour and others that haven't even started after an hour. It takes a lot to get us outside of our comfort zone. I have found two interesting things about comfort zones. First, as you spend time outside your comfort zone, your comfort zone actually expands. Second, and most important, God exists outside your comfort zone.

If we only surround ourselves with believers who look like us, we can subconsciously begin to think that God looks like us. If we only worship with believers who speak our language, we can forget that God is the Creator of the languages of the world. If we only worship with believers who like the same Bible verses we like, we can forget that the rest of the Bible exists for our correction, reproof, training, and equipping. If we consistently remain in our comfort zones, our God becomes increasingly small. But when we surround ourselves with Christians of different colors and sizes, we realize that we are all made in God's image and he is not made in ours. When we worship with believers who speak different languages, we realize that one language is not sufficient to describe our God. It is important that we stretch ourselves because it helps us realize that our God is bigger than we can imagine.

Many of the things we value in worship have to do with our own comfort. But a scriptural understanding of worship demands that we be uncomfortable at least *some* of the time in worship.

It is important that we become comfortable being uncomfortable. Comfort can be such an idol for us. Many of us pursue comfort at all costs. In fact, many of the things we value in worship have to do with our own comfort. But a scriptural understanding of worship demands that we be uncomfortable at least *some* of the time in worship.

Be Open

As multicultural worship leaders, we must embrace the truth that there is not one singular right way to "do" worship. This kind of openness does not come naturally to us as human beings but is a skill we must develop. Naturally, we think that the forms of worship and expression that work for us should work for everyone. This kind of thinking is ethnocentrism at its best, and it is in all of us, whether we like it or not. We as humans form habits, and we are not too crazy about change, particularly if we have been doing something the same way for a long time. When a community of people is made up of people of the same race, culture, and thought patterns, it is much easier to just assume that "the way we do it is the right way." Of course it is, and there is no one to challenge it! But in a multicultural worshipping community, it is not so simple.

Jesus clearly directs us to worship God in spirit and truth. But the forms that we use in worship (or even in church organizational structure) can change based on the context in which we find ourselves. Should we clap our hands? Sure! Should we silently reverence the Spirit through worship? Of course! Should we dance, pump our fists in the air, and hoot and holler? Why not! For multicultural worship leaders it is important to remember that worship expression can oftentimes be as individual as people are in general. And we must develop the skill of not only being okay with that but also actually inviting and encouraging it. Be open to singing to God loudly and softly. Be open to offering prayers to Jesus one at a time or all at the same time in different languages. Be open to pumping your fist in the air and getting your groove on during worship as well as spending time on your knees. You may need to practice some of these things on your own when no one else is around to help yourself become comfortable with new expressions. Be open to fresh ways to honor culture—your own and that of the people in your community—and be open to learning new ideas. Set the stage for a variety of worship expressions in the community you lead.

- Verbally give permission. Say things like, "If you'd like to dance in the aisles in praise to God, feel free. If you'd like to sit quietly and meditate on God's character, feel free."

- Help the people you lead see a variety of worship expressions in the Bible. Point them to psalms that talk about clapping hands and dancing and being still and bowing down.

- Let people from different cultures teach about worship. You might be surprised what Bible verses they choose to teach from. They may share things you have never considered!

Benefits of Stretching

As we grow older, our muscles gradually become tighter and shorter. This is the path of least resistance. This is our default. More and more, however, people are understanding that stretching is a vital part of health and fitness. It may or may not reduce the possibility of injury, but there are some proven benefits. So stretch those hamstrings!

1. Increased Circulation

Stretching increases the blood flow and therefore the supply of vital nutrients to cartilage and muscles. *How could stretching yourself culturally or liturgically enrich your life?* This increased supply of nutrients helps your muscles be less sore after working out. So, stretching on the front end and enduring some intentional discomfort can actually prevent some discomfort on the back end. Hmmm.

2. Flexibility

The main way to increase your flexibility is by stretching. Flexibility is extremely important for multicultural worship leaders. We must never fall into the trap that there is one right way to take an offering or play a song. You never know when you will need to use a violin to make sounds like an African harp or when your lead singer on a certain song will be twenty-five minutes late to the service. Increased flexibility allows you to exercise more easily. *How could stretching yourself culturally or liturgically help you do your job better or more easily?*

3. Increased Range of Motion

Stretching is a proven way of effectively increasing range of motion in your joints. Better range of motion means improved balance. Better balance means you are less likely to fall. Many times, our views of worship are skewed one way or another. We have two or three go-to verses about worship and ignore all the other biblical references. *How could stretching yourself culturally or liturgically help you have a more balanced approach to worship and ministry?*

4. Reduce Stress

Gentle stretching exercises causes tense muscles to relax. Tension can have negative effects on just about every part of your body, not to mention the people around you. I have found that because I stretch myself often, I have a lot less tension when I am in new or unfamiliar circumstances. *How could stretching yourself culturally or liturgically help you have a more relaxed approach to new ideas or circumstances?*

You Must Stretch Yourself

We believe that it is important that you lead *yourself* first. You are by far the hardest person for you to lead. But leading yourself first allows for authentic and compassionate leadership. Leading yourself first enables you to lead by example and not simply in theory.

You must stretch yourself to earn the right to stretch others. As a multicultural worship leader, you will spend a lot of your time stretching others. You will constantly be inviting people to step outside their comfort zones. This is a necessary part of leading a culturally diverse congregation. Everyone must learn new things. Everyone must take turns following. Everyone must learn to be uncomfortable sometimes. And you must lead the way. Please don't ask people to go where you are unwilling to go yourself. Stretch yourself first. Then, you can rest assured that you are not asking more from others than you are asking of yourself. I am constantly stretching other people, so much so that I have a reputation for it. But people know that I am not asking them to do something I am unwilling to do. Once, I learned a chorus in Romanian in front of the congregation and allowed them to see me being stretched alongside them. Often as leaders we feel like we have to have it all figured out, but the truth is that God can really use our vulnerability to encourage others as well.

You must stretch yourself so you can help others navigate the stretching process. Stretching is uncomfortable. And often, when we are uncomfortable, we react negatively. We lash out at others. We protect ourselves at all costs. We make excuses. As you, as a leader, work through these natural reactions yourself, it can give you more compassion for those you lead. And it can offer you insight as to how to help them work through their natural reactions to discomfort. Stretching has long-term positive benefits. As you push through the short-term discomfort and begin to experience some of the long-term benefits, you can encourage those you lead to persevere as well. You can tell them of the goodness that is to come. Often, when it is time to step outside my comfort zone, I don't feel like doing it. Sometimes, I want to stand on the edge and contemplate all the risks before taking the plunge. But that only makes things more difficult for me. One technique I have learned is to take a deep breath and then just go for it. It is amazingly simple and surprisingly helpful. I share that technique with others often, and it has proven very beneficial for many. Had I not gone through the stretching process myself (many, many times), I would not have discovered something practical that could help others.

You must stretch yourself in order to stay humble. When I submit to the leadership of others, I am admitting that I don't have all the answers. When I try a new way of doing something, I am confessing that I don't have a corner on the market. As a learner, I am dependent on others to help me and teach me. The posture of a learner is a posture of humility. And truly, the posture of worship is a posture of humility. As I mentioned earlier in this chapter, the Greek word that is most commonly translated as *worship* in the New Testament is "Proskuneo." It literally means "to bow and to kiss toward." Bowing is a humble position and is a picture of our rightful attitude in worship. Stretching ourselves and frequently stepping outside our comfort zones are great ways to cultivate humility. When I couldn't even clap along with the congregation at the Ethiopian Orthodox church, it was humbling. There were young children who were clapping, and here I was, with my degree in music, and I couldn't follow the pattern. It is hard to be prideful if I am constantly realizing how much more there is to know.

You must stretch yourself because this world is huge, and the diversity God has created is vast. As a multicultural worship leader, you may have mastered the ability to sing in Spanish. Your pronunciation is great, and you have even learned a few phrases in Spanish such as "Gloria a Dios" (Glory to God) or "Dios te bendiga" (God bless you). You may be feeling pretty good about your competence, and you should. Then, one day a couple from Sudan walks into your congregation, and in order to lead their hearts in worship, you have a lot more learning to do. I am constantly meeting people who speak languages I have never heard of. Here is the good news, however. Once you have stretched yourself to learn a new language or culture, it gets easier! Just the other day I was learning a song in Swahili with some friends. And one of them said, "I am amazed at how fast you are picking this up." I said, quite simply, "I do this every day." The more you do it, the easier it becomes.

Creative Ways to Stretch Yourself Culturally and Liturgically

1. Look around you. What ethnic groups are represented in your congregation already? What about the community around your church? Study these cultures.

    A. Learn the language.

    B. Research the cultures represented in your community at the library or on the Internet.

    C. Find places where people from other cultures gather in your community: parks, farmer's market, and so on.

    D. Spend time in those places with the people; talk with them, and maybe even interview them.

2. Visit other churches, specifically churches of other denominations and other ethnicities. Pay attention to how members worship. Seek to use the whole Bible (and not just your favorite verses) as the lens through which you see everything.

3. Make friends, and build an honest relationship with someone from another culture.

4. Learn how to make a meal from another culture by asking a friend to teach you.

5. Begin a Bible study group with participants from different cultures. Don't be the leader or teacher. Be a fellow learner.

6. Take a dance class or martial arts class or cooking class from another culture.

7. Listen to worship music in different languages and styles. (Even better, have a listening party during which friends of different ethnicities bring their favorite worship music and share it.)

8. Read a book about worship written by someone from another culture.

9. Go on a cross-cultural missions trip and take the opportunity to fellowship with other Christian worshippers.

Reflect

Are you asking others to stretch in ways that you are unwilling to stretch yourself?

What is one step you can take to stretch yourself culturally in this season of your life?

Chapter 9

Processing Change

The only thing constant is change. In a multicultural congregation, this is even more obvious. So, as a leader, what are you going to do about it?

Change Is Inevitable

It's going to happen whether we like it or not. Sometimes we're okay with that truth, and at other times it frightens us. Some change we can control. We like to change the thermostat when we are hot or cold. We like to change our clothes depending on our mood. We like changing our locations from hour to hour if we so choose, moving from one coffee shop to another when too many people begin to crowd the space. Some change is decided for us. The financial markets will continue to fluctuate, and global migration will continue to be a reality. Your children will continue to grow, and you aren't getting any younger. People will come and go both in your private world as well as your ministry life. You could be laid off or lose a loved one. The reality is, however, that these things can happen to us and change our worlds forever.

Our world is changing and will continue to change at a rapid pace with regard to race. The 2010 US census was eye-opening to many as we began to realize how hard it is for people to check only one box to define their race or culture. In fact, nine million Americans self-identified as being part of more than one race, which increased by about 32 percent since 2000. Thirty-two percent—that's the national average. But in some states, the multiracial population increased by 99 percent. Multiracial families like mine will visit your church. Is there a place for them? White people will want to know where they can serve. Will you create space for them? African American people may arrive in the front row. Will they feel safe? Both Asian and Hispanic Americans will come with their friends and families. Will they feel seen? Will they be considered? The "nations" are here! How will we respond? Change happens. Change can be devastating to you, or it can develop you. Change can cripple you or invite you to walk joyfully down new paths that have never existed before.

Walking New Paths

I (Josh) live in the multicultural community of Clarkston, Georgia. It is estimated that 75 percent of the people who live in my town were born outside the United States. A number of years ago, Clarkston was targeted as a good place to resettle refugees for many reasons. Clarkston exists within the bounds of the Metro-Atlanta public transportation system. There were lots of empty apartment complexes in our town, waiting to be filled. Georgia has a mild climate. And there are lots of sidewalks in Clarkston. In fact, there are sidewalks almost everywhere in Clarkston. Sidewalks are important to us. Congolese women walk to the store and carry groceries back to their homes on their heads. Nepali grandparents walk their grandchildren to and from the local elementary school. Burmese women walk down the sidewalk and pick weeds and grasses to use for food and for medicinal purposes. Six-year-old kids walk a mile of sidewalks to get to our School of the Arts classes on Saturday mornings (and sometimes in the rain!). Workers stand on the sidewalk waiting for public buses to take them to their jobs. There are sidewalks *almost* everywhere in Clarkston. But *not everywhere*. Clarkston hasn't always been a multicultural community. And to be honest, there were more than enough sidewalks for the people who used to live here. Because they drove their cars wherever they wanted to go. But the community is different now. We walk *everywhere*. And sidewalks are *not everywhere*.

So, here's what has happened. Over time, walking paths have developed on the side of the road. In places where there are no sidewalks, there are well-worn paths where sidewalks should be. No one asked for permission to develop these walking paths. No one went to the government officials and tried to cut through all the red tape to have sidewalks built. Someone just started walking. I wonder who it was. Maybe it was one of those grandparents who walked the same way to and from his or her grandchild's school day after day. Soon, others began to follow. And then others. In time, clearly marked, usable paths developed that mark the way from one place to another.

"Do not go where the path may lead,
go instead where there is no path
and leave a trail."
—Author Unknown[1]

Some of you are realizing that the context that you are in doesn't have enough paths to accommodate the diversity God has brought to you. Some of you are realizing that the paths you do have don't adequately reflect the breadth of what God is doing in your midst. Maybe you should sit down and talk to the powers that be. Maybe you should petition for more paths. Or maybe you should just start walking. In time, a way becomes a trail. And soon enough, that trail could be a path.

Reflect

Does your current ministry context have enough paths to accommodate the diversity God has brought to your congregation?

What is one step you can take today to blaze a new trail that needs to exist?

Change Takes Time

In roughly my second year leading the worship ministry, I (Nikki) had decided that a change needed to be made to one of our Sunday morning band rotations. There was a band member who was struggling for various reasons to learn and perform the music required for worship. I spent months considering what to do about this. I loved this man, and the last thing in the world that I wanted to do was make a decision that might cause him pain or make him feel embarrassed. However, it was clear that a change needed to happen. I sat with this man in the lobby at church after one of our services and shared with him the need for him to stop playing on Sundays. It was effective immediately. Needless to say, he was not happy about my decision. Our conversation

---

1. This passage is often attributed to Ralph Waldo Emerson but appeared earlier in the work of poet Muriel Strode.

lasted about three minutes, tops. It only took three minutes for him to become so angry with me that he stormed out of the lobby, making it clear that he was done with me as well as the church.

I was so confused and hurt after this happened. This was not my intention at all. I was even frustrated with God. My accusatory prayers usually sounded like this, "Lord, why did you let me do this if you knew this would happen?" About a year or so after this confrontation, I received an answer from the Lord to my question. "You didn't wait," he said. I was broken.

Patience is a virtue. One of the most wonderful things about being the lead steward of a ministry or organization is that many times God gives us a vision for the future before our people will see it. God uses a variety of tactics in order give leaders direction for those whom they lead. He may use dreams. He may use conferences. He may use people. His options are limitless. Maybe God is giving or has already given you a vision for multicultural ministry. You envision a ministry full of all types of people who are flourishing in a plethora of cultural expressions. You are fired up about it and, if you are honest, want to see it happen, like yesterday! This is one of the challenges of leadership. Because you see a vision for the future so clearly, you expect others to see it as quickly and clearly as you do. They won't. It is your job to help them. And that will take time.

This vision that you've been given will most likely require change to happen. Change to your budget. Change to your communication style. Change to your current structures. This is where patience is so critical. If we are not patient and careful, we can attempt to implement sweeping changes without giving our people a chance to consider, understand, prepare for, and process the changes. In the situation with the band member at my church, I knew that it was time for him to transition out. The issue was that I didn't allow that transition to happen. It was a firing. That was not my intention, but that is exactly how it felt to him. I had taken months to process this coming change. I didn't give him the opportunity to do the same. He only had three minutes.

> If we are not patient and careful, we can attempt to implement sweeping changes without giving our people a chance to consider, understand, prepare for, and process the changes.

Here are some strategies from Josh for leading change as you move toward multicultural worship:

1. *Help the people you lead see the need for change.* Help them become aware of the issues at hand. Nikki might have said to her team member, "I notice you've been having trouble learning the music lately. Have you noticed that?" Sometimes people can be so caught up in themselves that they are unaware of what is really happening or how they are affecting others. Sometimes people can be so focused on their smartphones that they don't see the world around them. Think for a moment, how did you become aware of the need for change? Maybe you were driving through your church's neighborhood and noticed that there are a lot of Hispanics living down the street. Why not take your worship team on a drive or walk through the neighborhood one night before or after rehearsal? Give them a chance to see what you see. If you met someone in your congregation and heard her story of racial oppression or of leaving her home country in search of a better life, maybe your leadership team needs to hear the same thing. If you traveled overseas and it expanded your heart for how God is worshipped in other cultures, maybe you need to take your band on a trip to another country. If people haven't had the same opportunities as you have, how could they get your vision? Remember, there was a time when you didn't get your vision. Help the people you lead see (and hear and feel) the need for change.

2. *Recognize that change will impact diverse people differently.* Some cultures love new things and are spontaneous. Some people don't have the phrase "We've always done it this way" in their vocabularies. Other cultures love tradition and value heritage immensely. They find comfort in same-ness. I (Josh) love to try new things. My wife values familiarity. When deciding on a restaurant, I have said before that I don't care where we go as long as it is some place new. To which she replied, "I don't care where we go, as long as it is some place familiar." As different as we are, we have never once considered that because of our differences we should go to separate restaurants. No, we find ways to work together. We

105

take turns choosing. She finds familiar things at new restaurants. I find new and different things at familiar restaurants. We process change differently but together. Find ways to help the people you lead enter into one another's process. Find ways for them to hear one another, know one another, defer to one another. And be intentional about talking to diverse people about the changes that are happening. If you only talk to the spontaneous, adventurous people about change, you might change way too quickly. Likewise, if you only talk to the cautious, thoughtful people, you might change way too slowly. Help people process change differently but together.

3. *Consider ahead the best ways to communicate change.* Maybe your band member would have a better chance at understanding you if you were sitting together in a coffee shop. The relaxed environment and a cup of coffee may take the pressure off. Rather than call him out in front of people in rehearsal, save the conversation for a time when you are away from other people, in order to help him feel like his reputation isn't being threatened. Usually you want to raise awareness of the issue when people aren't in the midst of the circumstance. Not only is the environment in which change is communicated important, but also the time of day, the time of year, and the language used. Let's say you are trying to introduce songs in other languages to your congregation and they are slow to sing along. You don't want to stop in the middle of the song and say, "You know what? You guys aren't singing just because you're uncomfortable. You just need to lay your pride down and start singing." *Please don't do that!* Instead, maybe a Sunday or two later, when it is appropriate, you might say, "Sometimes our pride keeps us from trying new things, like introducing ourselves to a visitor at church or even singing a song in a different language. As we sing the old hymn 'When I Survey the Wondrous Cross,' let's do what it says and 'pour contempt on all our pride,' asking God to make us willing to try new things."

4. *Rather than implementing a huge change overnight, help people prepare for the change that is coming.* Just because people are aware of the need for change and understand why change needs to happen,

it doesn't mean they are ready to change. Ever been aware of the fact that you needed to go on a diet? We need time to prepare for change. For example, maybe you believe that your church needs to go from multiple services to one service as a way of encouraging unity and diversity. Okay. Let's say you have helped your leaders understand the need for change and they get it. Great! But you are not there yet. Now it is time for you to help prepare the people for the change that is coming. That might mean having a one-on-one conversation with a member of your congregation and asking him, "What does this change mean for you?" You give him the opportunity to think through and verbalize how this change will impact him. And you get the chance to listen, which is always good. You might ask permission to share your conversation on a broader scale. If he agrees, then on the following Sunday morning, you might say, "I was having a conversation with so-and-so this week about the upcoming change to one service. He was telling me that he would be affected in these ways. Have you thought about how this change will affect you?" That gives the congregation the opportunity to think intentionally about their own connection to the change. And it helps them know that you care about how this change affects people. You might also gather your ministry leaders together and have a brainstorming session about what needs to happen practically in order to make the change from many services to one service. What do the individual ministries need to change? What support do they need from the staff or other leaders? Inviting diverse people into the process of preparing for change will not only make the process better but also help them be more invested in the changes that are happening.

5. *Give people opportunities to process as change is happening and after change has occurred.* Some people take time to process. They won't be able to imagine ahead of time how a change will affect them. They won't be able to put words to something for a while. So, make sure all along the way, there are opportunities for dialogue. Ask such questions as, "What do you think is going well in this process?" "What have you been surprised by in

this process?" "What challenges have you faced in this process?" Don't be afraid to bring things up. Don't be afraid to ask questions and then simply listen. If you don't know how to respond, you can simply thank them for sharing their thoughts with you. Their perspective is a gift to you as a leader (whether it feels like one or not). It might be helpful to have some open unstructured dialogue around a meal. It might be helpful to have a church meeting for people to share their perspectives and hear from one another. It might be helpful for the people who are enjoying the change to know that there are others who are having a hard time. And it might be helpful for those who are having a hard time with change to know that there are others who are enjoying it.

Leadership and Farming

In Matthew 13:1-24, Jesus tells a story about a farmer and the seed that he plants. Consider that your vision for a more diverse ministry is like a seed and the hearts of the people you are leading, the soil.

Some seeds fall on soil that is not ready to receive the message. It was just sort of thrown on the soil with no planning or care, so it never germinates. Some seeds fall on soil that is a little rocky, maybe even hard-hearted toward the work of racial inclusiveness. It is received but then "doesn't take" because the roots did not grow deep. Once life or ministry gets a little hard, there is a failure in relationship, or someone leaves, the people you are leading could feel as though "this diversity stuff doesn't work." Other seeds fall on soil that is initially ready to receive, but then all too quickly, the message of racial integration ends up on a list with everything else that one has to do in a given season. The thought of adding one more thing to the list is exhausting, and like other items on that list, it is never achieved.

Remember that there are all types of soil within the community around you. Do all you can to prepare the soil of your people's hearts for the seed that you are about to plant. The seed is good, but if you plant it too soon or plant too much of it all at one time, when the soil is not prepared, we run the risk of it producing frustration and not fruit. Just like you would lead people through a new building project, a capital campaign, a new evangelism initiative, or new community project, you need to shepherd them through this new way of thinking and responding with regard to diversity. Even if your ministry or organization is currently racially and culturally diverse, in order for your people to move to even greater expressions of diversity, they will need to be communicated with and shepherded through the process of change. Be sure to prepare them for what is to come before planting those seeds.

Reflect

Identify what type of soil you are currently tilling. Have you prepared it for the new seed?

Considering the ideas regarding how to help your people process change, write out a plan for how you will communicate and execute the change you desire to make. Once you have written out the process, share it with diverse people (some who like change, some who don't like change, people with different cultural perspectives, and so on) and be open to their feedback.

★ ★
★

Chapter 10

Making Room for Diversity

Your ministry team must *be diverse. This does not happen naturally,*
however. Make sure you are structuring and restructuring for diversity.

People crave authenticity. This is especially true regarding worship in the
church. Worship magazines devote entire issues to the subject. We pursue
authenticity as leaders, and we require it of those we lead. All too often,
however, it seems as though an essential piece of our authenticity is missing
among some worship ministries within multicultural churches. This truth
became glaringly obvious during a workshop that Josh and I taught at a national conference. The title of the workshop was "Building and Sustaining a
Healthy Multiethnic Worship Ministry." The room was filled with roughly
forty people who were either leading in multicultural churches or leading in
uni-cultural churches with a desire to see more racial diversity represented
in their congregations. We began with this simple question: "How many of
you in this room would say that the church where you lead worship is truly
multicultural?" About 90 percent of the people in the room raised their hands
high. We were delighted at that response! The next question was this: "How
many of you in this room would say that the worship ministry where you lead
or serve appropriately represents the cultural diversity in your church?" The
response was unexpected. About 10 percent of the people in the room raised
their hands. Why was this so? Can a multicultural church communicate authenticity if there are ministries or leadership structures in the church that
are not culturally diverse? And how does this even happen in the first place?
A uni-cultural ministry in a multicultural church will, in time, undermine.

A uni-cultural ministry in a multicultural church will, in time, undermine.

Ministry is all about the people. One of the things that I (Nikki) love about leading multicultural worship and multicultural people is that it is impossible to do it alone. Josh always says, "No one person can be diverse in himself." The bottom line is that we need one another. It is *imperative* that we build teams that are ethnically diverse. In addition, consider other diverse characteristics such as gender, age, language, and race. Consider hearing and Deaf populations as well. If you are going to be a multicultural leader, you must develop the skill of learning to be inclusive of as many different types of people as possible. Learn how to relate to different people yourself and also how to help diverse people relate to one another. Build teams of musicians who can play different styles of music.

As leaders of dynamic, multicultural worship ministries, the opportunity for our teams to reflect the already-existing diversity of the body of Christ will be ever before us. The Apostle Paul says in Ephesians 4:11-12 that the responsibility given to pastors, teachers, and leaders is to "equip God's people for the work of serving and building up the body of Christ." You have been given that responsibility if you are in leadership. As a leader in a multicultural church, you have been given the unique privilege to work hard at pursuing and growing racially and culturally diverse teams. Many times, a worship or creative arts ministry will feel a larger burden than other ministries within the church to build diverse teams simply because it is one of the most visible ministries within the church. Consider this responsibility not as a burden but as an opportunity.

Strategies for Diversifying Worship Ministries

The following are tested and proven strategies that can ensure that you will always have the heart to engage people and the tools to diversify your teams.

Strategy #1: Go, Get Them: Build Diverse Teams of People

During an e-mail exchange with a leader in a multiethnic church, I (Nikki) asked the question, "So how's it going?" This brother, who is a worship pastor, began to share his frustration with me about how tough it was to find non-White people to play in the band. He mentioned how he did not know how to find people to serve within the ministry and had the added pressure of a directive by his senior pastor to increase his team's ethnic diversity. He confessed that he felt that if there were people in the church who had those gifts that they would "come forward" and want to serve.

When you are a leader in a multicultural church, you may need to let go of "traditional" philosophies of ministry. Consider this: your traditional approach to ministry is what has gotten you where you are. If you want to have something different from what you already have, you may need to change your approach. Oftentimes, as ministry leaders, we wait for people to contact us and tell us that they wish to serve. However, chances are that if we do that, we will only get one type of person and who will most likely be people who look like us. At Bridgeway, where I lead, if I waited for every person to come to me to join the team, I would have several teams made up of all African American females.

Don't wait for people to come to you. You go and get them! Go and find the diversity that you want to see in your ministry. It is also important to realize that volunteering in a church may come more naturally for some cultures than for others. For instance, for some African American women who have grown up in church, volunteering and showing up at events is natural for them. It has always been a part of their church history. There is a history of service within the African American church, and to serve is to be a part of that church community. (Again, these are broad generalizations and not every African American woman will respond this way, but it does happen in many circumstances.) In contrast, because of their collective mind-set, people from certain Asian cultures may never volunteer. They may be extremely uncomfortable promoting themselves, speaking of their own abilities, and volunteering to be a part of the worship ministry. In many cases, you, being the leader, may need personally to extend an invitation to people in that culture and draw them out. Think about this for a minute: can you imagine what it might feel like for someone in your congregation to get a personal and direct invite from you, the leader of that ministry? An invitation rather than an open call for volunteers can be a powerful thing. Be sure to have a variety of tools and vehicles at your disposal in which to draw people in and invite them to be a part of what God is doing within the ministry that you lead.

Volunteering in a church may come more naturally for some cultures than for others.

Are you lacking Korean and Indian representation? Are African Americans missing from your band? Are Caucasian and Hispanic brothers and sisters sitting in your congregation, but not serving in your ministry? Do you have anyone over the age of sixty or under the age of twenty singing on your vocal team? These are the questions that you should grapple with as a leader in a multicultural church or ministry. Remember, think consideration and not quotas! Do not choose the path of least resistance. Go and invite a diverse group of people to serve alongside you.

Reflect

Think of your ministry and the people in it right now. Does the worship ministry at your church appropriately reflect the diversity that is currently at your church or reflect the diverse community that you would like to be?

Who might you need to extend a personal invitation to in order to more fully represent God's desire for the nations to worship him together?

Strategy #2: Redefine the Qualifications

During a conversation with a fellow leader, I (Nikki) asked him about the lack of diversity in the ministry that he leads. He is a leader in a multicultural church; however, the ministry that he led at the time consisted of mostly African American men. I asked him about this, and he said that the men on his team were the ones who approached him with a desire to serve and who were the best qualified. First of all, notice that they "approached him." Again, this could be a cultural phenomenon. In addition, the fact that there are only African American men serving in this ministry could communicate in the minds of some that only this group of people is qualified and does it the best.

So, who is it that you are looking for? When you think about the kinds of people whom you would like to add to your team, do you consider diversity as well as skill? This can be a tricky thing to define, particularly when you are defining it for a ministry that relies so much on specifically skilled people to accomplish a goal. Many times, for creative people like us, when we seek out people for our teams, the first thing we look for is skill, and who can blame us, right? I mean, if you are looking for a piano player, you need to find someone who actually can play the piano! But is that the only criteria? Don't we also look for people who know Christ and who are committed to our churches? In a multicultural church, if your teams are not racially and culturally diverse, I would venture to say that they are not successful.

A lack of diversity within our music ministries is one of the biggest issues facing our multicultural churches today. It's hard! But do you know that God knows exactly who you need at any given time? Have you ever prayed and asked God for a diverse team? Jesus, before he chose his disciples, spent all night in prayer! And in Matthew 6:8, he even reminds his disciples that the "Father knows what you need before you ask." Remember that God sees everything and knows your need. Since diversity is God's idea anyway, remember that he will graciously give us what we need to accomplish the good works that were planned in advance for us (and our ministries) to do.

Reflect

What are the qualifications necessary within your current context to create teams that are skilled as well as diverse?

Based on what God has given you right now, what is one thing that you can do as a leader to meet that goal?

Strategy #3: Hold Loosely to Your Structure or Process

Be willing to change your structure or style of ministry based on whom God brings to your church and what you determine is needed for a diverse ministry. For years at Bridgeway, the way that someone would become a member of the worship ministry was to seek out the ministry leader at the time and simply say that she was interested. If she was a singer, she would be invited to join the choir, and if she played an instrument, she was invited to sit in with the band. One of the things that I appreciated about this approach was that it was extremely inclusive and allowed people in our congregation to become involved in the ministry without many hoops to jump through or "red tape" to deal with. The challenges with this approach were many.

First, this approach provided no way for us to evaluate a person's skill. Second, there was no way to even know if someone was, indeed, a Christ-follower. Third (and most important for our current discussion), it was hurting our ethnic diversity. Having seen these challenges for years under previous leadership, I (Nikki) decided to institute an audition process. The word *audition* can bring up many different emotions depending on one's own experience and even given one's cultural background. There were cultures in our church that naturally responded to (in my opinion) the more extroverted approach of "just come out, meet the leader, and start serving." However, I had a theory that for other cultures within our church, this approach could be perceived as having no definite structure. I believed that some cultures needed more of a structured "on ramp" in order to feel like they were becoming a part of something. And, quite frankly, some cultures are used to going through an assessment of some kind to determine eligibility for serving, particularly within a ministry that is music focused.

At first, I received some push back from those who were concerned that instituting auditions would make people feel like they were on *American Idol* or that the focus was all about the skill and not the person. I had a different vision completely. I had a vision for creating an audition process that was both highly relational as well as intentionally structured so as to speak to different cultural interpretations and experiences. Having both of these things integrated into an audition process presented an opportunity for great things to happen—at least the way I saw it.

To make a long story short, since we have incorporated the audition process into the framework of our ministry, we have seen a dramatic increase in the cultural diversity. I believe that this is, in part, because of a restructured process on the front end that allows many cultures to feel comfortable with a formal "sign-up" as well as to have the assurance of feeling like a connected community along the way. Additionally, I have a tremendous opportunity now to bring my diverse leaders in on this process. Auditions are our favorite time of year around Bridgeway because of what God has been doing through it.

So why do I share this with you? Many times we can get so used to the way that we've always done things within our ministries that we forget that we may have other options and alternatives available to us. Don't be afraid to change your organizational structures and create new structures for the sake of ethnic and cultural diversity. It is quite possible that there are existing structures that have been in place for years that could be hurting your efforts to diversify your ministry. If diversity is the goal, then all structures and systems need to work toward that goal. Don't fear this. See it as an opportunity for the Lord (and your church) to do something new. You're a Creative, right? So, be creative and allow the structures that you put in place to communicate inclusiveness and community.

It is quite possible that there are existing structures that have been in place for years that could be hurting your efforts to diversify your ministry.

Here are a couple of practical ways (from Josh) that we have altered some structures to make them fit our multicultural community:

1. Intentional "connecting time" at the beginning of events. When we have meetings, gatherings, and rehearsals, we intentionally schedule the first few minutes (up to thirty minutes) of the gathering for intentional connecting with one another. This may be structured (like a Bible study or prayer time) or unstructured (like mingling or eating together). This allows people who are more event oriented to arrive a few minutes late without missing the content of the meeting. It also helps those who are not as relational to have time and space carved out for them to develop relationships.

2. Culture-shaped communication. I communicate on different schedules for different cultures. I tend to give my White American teachers (who are often planners) a month's notice so they can get events on their calendars ahead of time. I tend to ask my African immigrant teachers the week of an event, as they are likely to feel more comfortable with that time frame. I found that it causes stress to certain teachers if I ask them too late, and for others, asking them too early brings tension.

Be creative. Figure out structures and processes that honor the different cultures in your midst. Figure out things that work for your community. And feel free to try something for a while and if it doesn't work, change it.

> **Reflect**
>
> Are you doing ministry in a particular way just because it's always been done that way?
>
> What structures could you change or add that might increase your racial diversity?
>
> Some ideas and areas to consider are:
>
> Rehearsals: Timing, structuring of services, having community time versus task-oriented time, using translators for those who do not speak the primary language
>
> Planning: Including others, asking for help, planning enough in advance for people to become involved, planning with diverse people in mind
>
> Music: Utilizing various genres, learning music from those in your congregation, including language during your worship set.

Why Bother?

Pursuing and growing a racially and culturally diverse worship ministry will *give your ministry credibility* among your church community and the community outside the walls of your church. A monocultural ministry within a multicultural church will in time undermine the vision. If every ministry within the church would take up the charge to make room for diverse people groups and cultures within their ministries, it will truly become a community that is not just multicolored, but truly multicultural. Your credibility will also rise within the community where your church is located because your ministry will be equipped to minister to and understand many of the different types of people in your neighborhood.

Pursuing and growing a racially and culturally diverse worship ministry will *equip your ministry with multiple musical and cultural perspectives on worship in the church*. You will be opened to more than just one style, one genre, one tool to use in order to reach people for Christ and build up the body of Christ. You and your ministry teams will become more equipped to go into just about any situation, any culture, or any ethnic church and have a level of openness, exposure, and comfort that will help you lead a variety of people groups more effectively.

Pursuing and growing a racially and culturally diverse worship ministry will also *reinforce the vision of the church as a whole.* As worship leaders, we have a great opportunity to leverage the people-resources that God has given us as well as the platforms we have to model the importance of diversity in music, culture, and relationship. Our role as leaders—of being intentional with the people we invite to participate in our ministries—is crucial to the health and diversity of the church as a whole.

Making room for diversity in your ministry is not always easy, but it very well could be some of the most meaningful work that you do as a leader within your growing diverse church.

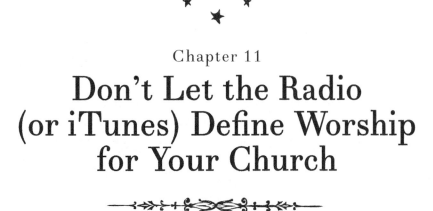

Chapter 11

Don't Let the Radio (or iTunes) Define Worship for Your Church

Your church is unique. You should sound like it. Mainstream doesn't always work in multicultural worship, and that's okay.

"As the Deer" Is Old. So What? So Is "How Great Thou Art"!

Have you ever found yourself having a conversation with someone who loves to define the worth of a song based on how "old" it is? No? Well you must not know any hip worship leaders. I (Nikki) had a worship pastor friend tell me once that he refused to sing the song "As the Deer" because it was old and irrelevant. Some of you reading this chapter have never even heard of the song "As the Deer." That's okay; it's old. I'm kidding—sort of. I asked him what kind of songs he was singing in his church and how he went about choosing worship music for his community. He told me the way his church functions is that they keep an eye on the top five worship songs on iTunes in any given season, and then those are the songs that they will do. Once a song moves off of that list, then they take it out of rotation in their church and that is how they know that a song is still relevant for their community. This was the first time that I had heard someone verbalize his strategy this way. I will say that since having that conversation with my friend, I have noticed more and more worship leaders employing the same strategy. There are dangers for worship leaders who decide to use iTunes and Christian radio alone to lead them in choosing music for their community and to inform their opinions on what is considered "new," "old," "relevant," or "irrelevant."

Right now, many churches are allowing the radio to determine what is good or not so good for their churches to sing. There are many leaders who are looking at the top-five songs on the iTunes Christian charts and allowing that information alone to determine what they will sing in their churches. There are many leaders who believe that this will be the way that they stay relevant. Relevant to whom? Who are you trying to reach? This strategy might work really well within monocultural churches. If you are a church of predominantly White people, it is possible (though still unlikely, interestingly) that they are all listening to the CCM station, which stands for Contemporary Christian Music, which if you look closely usually means "White rock music." If you find yourself in a predominantly African American church, you may find that the majority of people listen to the gospel station, which is usually code for "Black Jesus music" that is sung by choirs and really talented musicians. And if you find yourself in a Hispanic church or a Korean church or a Jamaican church, you can find stations that will play music in any language and genre that you are looking for. But if you are reading this book, chances are you are in a church community that is at least somewhat culturally diverse (or hopes to be), and the traditional way that monocultural churches approach choosing music may not work for you. There is nothing inherently wrong with the songs that you hear on the radio; they usually play a specific genre of music (that is "heart music" for specific people), and that could be why they are so popular. But I want to encourage you, as a leader within a multicultural context, do not rely on the radio when you are choosing music that is appropriate for your church. I want to give you permission to be creative, authentic, and unique in your approach to music.

Be Aware

- The songs playing on the radio likely have money and record labels behind them.

- The radio is racially segregated. By taking our cues from the radio, we could be following these patterns of segregation without even knowing it.

- Young people buy the most music and therefore often the top five songs in any given genre appeal to the younger people. Consider the older members of your congregation as well.

- Songs that are getting lots of airplay and media attention will be on CCLI (Christian Copyright Licensing International), with a chart and a recording. It's convenient. But you only get one type of music. CCLI has mostly White CCM music.

I (Nikki) was on the phone with a friend who is a White worship pastor and who was struggling along with his African American worship leader to find the "right" songs for their worship services. I asked him what the main issue was. His answer was relevance. I asked him to tell me more. He proceeded to tell me how they just couldn't agree on what songs were culturally appropriate for services. Both pastors were concerned with being "relevant." The White pastor began to tell me that his main issue was that the African American worship leader was bringing songs to the table from years past, old songs by gospel singer Fred Hammond and the group Commissioned. I asked him why that was a problem. He replied that he would be fine with old songs if they were "classics" like Steve Miller Band. My question to him was, "Classic to whom?" As leaders who live, breathe, and move in a multicultural environment, it is important to remember that the definition of relevance varies from culture to culture within your community.

The definition of relevance varies from culture to culture within your community.

If the current, most popular worship band redid the song "As the Deer," I'll bet you that many churches in your city would be covering that song all of the sudden. Things have relevance once people ascribe relevance to them. If you are not careful, the music you hear on the radio will dictate to you the *structures* of your church as well. How many people should be on the worship team? Should you have a choir? Should you have a string section? No, because everything on the recording is electric guitar and drums. This is a *danger*. Don't let the radio dictate what you do with your worshipping community. In a multicultural environment, mainstream doesn't always work because multi-cultural ministry is not mainstream. So then, how do you choose what your church will sing in a multicultural community?

Don't allow the radio to take the place of the Holy Spirit when you choose music. What is the reason you choose the songs that you do? If your goal is relevance alone, I would like to encourage you to go deeper than that. Here are a few questions to consider when you are deciding on which songs to sing at your next worship gathering.

1. What should we sing in this season of our church?
2. What is the Holy Spirit impressing on my own heart as a person and a leader?
3. Where do I want to lead the congregation?
4. What does our diverse congregation need to express to God?

The Bridgeway Sound

Bridgeway was founded as a multicultural church. We have never been mainstream. And the music at Bridgeway has always been diverse in terms of genre and also in terms of the people who are creating it and leading it. I inherited this value system from the leaders who came before me. We strive to be a creative ministry. We recognize that multicultural worship leaders are trailblazers, creating things that do not yet exist. We don't want to simply reproduce something that has already happened. And, to be honest, we can't reproduce recordings exactly on Sunday mornings. It is impossible to sound like the recording because most people are working with a team of volunteers with different skill levels. The professional recording has tuning, backup singers, four electric guitar tracks, synth sounds tucked into the mix, and so on. I see people trying to reproduce that sound exactly and getting frustrated when they can't. Truth be told, the *artist* cannot even reproduce the sound on his own album. So, stop trying. Once you realize that you cannot reproduce something, instead of finding frustration, you can find freedom. Someone else already did it that way. You be you. I certainly hope you sound different! You are not a machine. Your worship team is not made up of robots. My fear for the church is that we will become just an eternal cover band. Artists in churches have more to offer than just reproducing what has already been done.

Artists in churches have more to offer than just reproducing what has already been done.

Early on, we made a decision about who we wanted to become as a worship ministry. We want to be a ministry that is for everybody, a ministry that is safe. People matter; they should be seen and not have to check their culture at the door. The beauty of a multicultural experience is that everybody brings their own experiences and perspectives to the table. We use music to model this idea of collaboration very practically.

We value creativity. If we do the same song four weeks in a row, hopefully that song sounds the slightest bit different because the people are different. We want every live experience to be something new and fresh. We look for God to do something new in each new space. This is the fun and beauty of making music together.

Another Bridgeway characteristic is intentionally determining who we are as a ministry. Decide who you want to be. Decide what you will value as a worship ministry. If you don't make the decision, then someone will make it for you. Make your own decisions based on where the Holy Spirit is leading you and what he is doing within your community. Your values will drive what you do. Choose your parameters wisely.

We have always been diverse in genre and in musicians and singers. But we have also been constantly changing. When talking about worship services, people who come to Bridgeway often say, "You never know what you're going to get!" Our church today should not sound like it did ten years ago. There are new people here. People have come, and people have left. That should affect the sound. And the people who have been part of our church for the last ten years have been growing and developing, and God has been changing them. So even they should sound different than they did ten years ago.

The Bridgeway sound has morphed over the years and continues to. The Black people in church would say we sound more White than Black. And the White people would say we sound more Black than White. As a leader, I think that those kinds of comments are a good sign that we are right where we need to be. I would say that we are strongly influenced by R & B and jazz, and our church's history contributes to this. We made decisions early on to leverage these genres that are inherently multicultural and cross-cultural. Our primary instrument is usually keyboard, not guitar, as the versatility of the keyboard suits us well. That affects our sound. We often take songs that were made popular in other genres and rearrange them. We may add some color (seconds and sevenths and ninths for you musical theory people) to the chords. We may slow the groove down and give it a bit of "neck." We have learned over the years how to make songs sound and feel like us.

Bridgeway Language

In the last few years, we have morphed significantly by incorporating different languages into our worship services. Now, it is a part of who we are as a community of worshippers. When describing church to others, our members say, "We sing in different languages like Spanish, Yoruba, and Korean." Our congregants sometimes invite people to our church by saying, "We sometimes sing in your language." What a beautiful way to let people know we are considering them even before they step into the doors of our church.

> ## Our congregants sometimes invite people to our church by saying, "We sometimes sing in your language."

Bridgeway Choir

We have a choir at Bridgeway that leads worship regularly. Lots of churches are getting rid of their choirs because "popular" worship songs are not written for choirs, and what people hear on the radio does not include a choir. I have friends who have gotten rid of a one-hundred-voice choir because it is not "cool" anymore.

So, you hear a song that you love on the radio. It is one lead vocalist and one background singer. You love the song, but you have a choir. How can you translate that song and make it work in your context? Do you make the choir sit down on this song and find a soloist and background singer? Or do you change up the song to make it work for the choir? I rearrange songs every month when our choir sings. First, I think, "Who do I have in my choir?" Second, I think, "What does my choir sound like?" I think about the key of the song. If we do it in the same key as the recording, can my men's section belt it out at the top of their voice? If not, maybe I can change the key. Or, if I can't change the key for some reason, then I ask, "What part of the song can I create so the men's section can minister in their sweet spot?" I will create an entire new section of a song (maybe a vocal arrangement vamp for instance) for my choir so they can sing in their sweet spot. I know that I can cut the instruments out and the choir will rise to the occasion. *I know my choir.* When my choir guys have their own distinct melody or counter-melody, they come to life! There is *always* a way to morph something to fit your people. Develop your own abilities to rearrange. Or, ask for help. You might ask other leaders in other churches or people within your own congregation. There is always a way to rearrange!

There is *always* a way to morph something to fit your people.

We are constantly creating something that does not yet exist. So, we can't point to the radio recording and say, "We will know when the product is ready when it sounds like that." What does our community sound like right now? And what do we want the sound of our community to be? That can only be found by allowing our people to fill in the blanks.

Who Fills in the Blanks?

Many people believe the leader needs to have all the ideas, all the vision, all the answers. This is absolutely not true. And leaders with all the answers can actually be damaging to the souls of the people they lead. They can kill all creativity and imagination in short order.

The leader's job is to provide enough structure so the people have rails to run on, but not too much structure that the people have no room to bring their own voice. I often send my team demo recordings that are very simple. The recording may have just the vocal and a piano accompaniment. That leaves room for the drummer and the saxophone player and even the harmony singers to "fill in the blanks" at rehearsal. Sometimes, I send a demo and say, "Here's the original recording. But I want it to feel funkier and groovier than this." I give ideas such as, "Can you play long notes on that section rather than more rhythmic notes?" However, I don't micromanage and tell people exactly what to play.

> # The leader's job is to provide enough structure so the people have rails to run on, but not too much structure that the people have no room to bring their own voice.

I ask for ideas. The leader doesn't have to fill in the blanks. Instead, she should specifically leave blanks for other people to fill in. Be careful not to send the message of "Don't bring your ideas here. We are doing it this way." If you are someone who has lots of answers, you will have to make space for others ideas. Use your ideas as a backup plan. But don't reveal them too soon. Let there be time and space for even the more introverted, processor-type people to have a chance to respond.

What Not to Say

1. *"We are going to do this exactly like the recording."*

Talk about pressure. And this language says that you might as well have robots who can simply mimic and re-create sounds rather than have unique human beings created to be creative in the image of God.

2. *"That's not the right way to do this song."*

Many people believe that there is one right key in which to sing a song. But what if that key doesn't work for your singers? Or, what if your guitarist can't play in B-flat?

3. *"Can you play that line like so-and-so plays it?"*

This isn't so-and-so's week to play. What you create each week is unique to the community that is there that week. And that's good. Musicians already struggle greatly with comparing themselves to one another. Make sure your language gives them no fuel for this destructive behavior.

4. *"This is the way we've always done it."*

Who is "we" anyway? We are different than we were last week or last year. We might do the same song two weeks in a row, the first week as a techno song and the next week as a CCM, guitar-strumming song. Both musical styles speak to people in our congregation. There is a sense then that both are uniquely "us."

What to Say

1. *"I know I want to change this song up, but I'm not sure what will work. Who has an idea?"*

This helps people understand that you need their creativity. It gives opportunity for them to bring something unique from their own imagination. Someone may play a few chords, and then the next thing you know, the band is in a groove. That happens in community. And what is created in that specific moment of time, and in that specific community, is completely unique. It could never be re-created by a different group of people. Everyone is influencing it somehow, even by just being in the room or by saying, "I like that," or "Ooh, that's nice."

2. *"Let's just try it!"*

Our church culture, not just in the worship realm, embraces this approach. There is no harm in trying. And even if it doesn't work, maybe it will lead us to something that does work. Or, maybe we will learn something. Or, maybe we will all have an opportunity to laugh at how ridiculous we just looked or sounded. There is freedom to fail.

3. *"Let's create something new!"*

Notice the language of inclusion. The different people and culture and musical backgrounds they bring affect the sound. We value creativity and experimentation. Our church culture (not just in the worship realm) is one of "just try it!" freedom to fail, not "this is the way we have always done it." Let's create something new. Let's do our own thing. If someone has an idea, we fan the flame of the idea. We don't perceive someone's idea as a threat. Sometimes it works and sometimes it doesn't. That's okay!

4. *"Feel free to figure out your own part."*

This kind of language helps reinforce the idea that everyone has something to offer. It affirms that you believe in the person's ability. I have chosen to believe that each one of my team members is capable and has something valuable to offer. That's why God has brought them to this church. Each person has something important to contribute to the sound of our community.

Reflect

In your ministry, what is the forum for people to share their song or arrangement ideas? What is the "safe" space and time for them to bring up their ideas?

Do you provide both structured and unstructured (or less structured) times for your team to be together for such things to happen?

Unstructured (or Less Structed) Moments

1. *Make Room for Creativity.*

Each week, the offering song is our slot for band creativity. Our band director always has a plan but asks others for ideas. Sometimes, he asks people ahead of time to bring ideas. Sometimes he asks them on the spot in rehearsal. Some people need this advanced notice for creativity. Some people do their best creating spontaneously. Every week, the offering is a collaborative moment that sounds and feels unique.

2. *Build a room for natural community.*

Sunday morning, between services, is prime relational time. We are together in the green room (actually, it is orange), which was designed for the purpose of providing a place for our teams to rest, relax, and recharge. We eat together. Catch up with one another. We hang out together. Sundays are long days for us because we normally arrive somewhere between 6:15 and 6:30 in the morning and usually don't leave until close to 2:00 p.m. There is a lot of time to just be together. Our green-room time is not mandatory or required by any means, but it has become our team's place to hang out on Sundays. It has become a lovely place of unstructured relational time where teams that serve can catch up with one another on life. If you walk by the tables of people or pass by the comfy couches or the food table, you may hear people talking about everything from politics and work to family and faith. You may hear people praying for one another or laughing at a really stupid joke. You may see people leaning into serious conversations being held almost at a whisper. And let's be honest, since we get there really early in the morning, you will more than likely see napping—lots of napping.

3. Sacrifice rehearsal time for connection time.

Community time around (or outside of) rehearsals has been a life-giver for our ministry. Before we play or sing a note, we gather together, look one another in the eye, share scripture together, pray, relate, and catch up. *Rich worship flows out of rich community.* Whether it is a band jam at someone's house instead of on your platform, watching a DVD of some music, or having food, just play together. Go see shows together. I take people with me when I teach workshops other places and when I lead worship other places. More times than not, we have dance parties before choir rehearsal. No, I'm not making that up!

Rich worship flows out of rich community.

Closing Story

During one of the times that Josh had come to Maryland to minister with us at Bridgeway, I (Nikki) decided to take some of my band guys out for lunch to spend time with him after our worship service. Sitting around a table at our favorite Cuban restaurant here in town with some of the best people I know was a real gift. What happens when you get a bunch of Creatives around a table? Yes. We talk about music—lots of it! Rod, one of my percussion players, said out of nowhere, "I am learning to play the didgeridoo." Intrigued, I asked him to tell me more. He said that he had been working to expand his percussion gifts and had always been fascinated with that instrument and the physical demand that was required. Then he said, "I have always wanted to play it for worship, but I am not sure where it would fit." My response to him was, "We will make it fit!"

Over the next week or so, I just kept thinking, *how can we use this didgeridoo*? The next time Rod was scheduled to be on the Sunday morning worship rotation, I happened to find a song that was in the same key as the didgeridoo. After a little creative arranging and musical road-mapping, we rearranged the song musically so that Rod could begin the song, highlighting the sound of the didgeridoo. Then, the guitar came in over the drone. Then, in the musical interludes, we focused on the didgeridoo again. Then, we ended the song with didgeridoo and drums. We created a "buzz" among the people, and the smile on Rod's face all morning long was contagious. All morning long, I kept getting the question from people in the congregation, "What was that instrument?" I had not considered the fact that so many people would be as intrigued as I was about this new instrument they heard and saw on stage. The most encouraging thing was that when people asked me about the didgeridoo, I was afforded the opportunity to educate people not only about the instrument, but also about the cultural significance of that particular instrument in Aborigine culture. Even more significant for community-building, I got to tell them the story about how I found out that Rod played the didgeridoo while sitting around with my team having Cuban food. It was a wonderful opportunity to teach but also to add value to my friend, Rod, who was learning a new skill. The beginning of this memorable moment happened over lunch in an unstructured time. If the only time you are with your people is in structured environments, you might never know that your team member even plays the didgeridoo. And he might never even think to bring it up in a structured environment.

Opportunities like this can be missed if we are not open and diligent in our quest to find out what is "our" sound. When was the last time you've heard a didgeridoo in a worship song on the radio? I don't think I have ever heard that. Never forget that God has led your people to your church or ministry for a reason. They have gifts that your church needs. It is our job as leaders to help them find out how to best utilize those gifts within the context of our community. You have a sound. Your church has a sound. When your ministry gets together to play music, they have a sound. Find out what it is. And when you do, hold fast to the values of that sound, and don't ever let the radio define what is best for you. The Holy Spirit will lead you into all truth. It is who he is and what he does. Trust that he will reveal to you the sound that is supposed to come out of your diverse community. Trust that it will not sound exactly like the church down the road, the church getting all the press on TV, or your favorite Christian artist. Remember, you have permission to be creative and to do whatever you can to make your music sound like the worshipping community that you *are* and who you *want to be*. What a fun adventure!

Reflect

How do you find your congregation's unique sound?

Listen to a lot of music (and not just the radio station). Can you hear your congregation singing certain things? You are what you listen to. Listen intently when you get together and play music. What is coming out? What kind of styles? What does your team resonate with? When do they come alive? Talk to your people within the ministry and your congregation. Ask diverse people for music suggestions. What are people listening to? What is moving them?

Consider how your music might morph according to the core values of your ministry.

Consider the skill level of your team. What are their unique strengths and weaknesses? How can your music leverage your team's strengths?

If you are doing a song that has previously been recorded, how could you change up the recording to make it sound more like you? Here are a few ideas:

Use different instrumentation to cater it to your context.

Infuse language and translate some songs. Don't use Google to translate!

Take a popular worship song and have someone write and insert a rap into the song. Or put the song in a medley with a song of a totally different style or genre.

Sing a cappella.

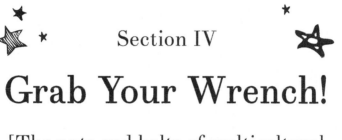

Section IV

Grab Your Wrench!

[The nuts and bolts of multicultural
worship leading]

Chapter 12

Who and What Do You Have?

Rather than focusing on what you don't have, take stock of the people, talents, languages, and cultural resources that are already in your congregation.

What Is in Your Hand?

A few years ago, I (Josh) had the opportunity to travel to Cuba in an effort to connect Cuban congregations with congregations in Florida. I was an ambassador of sorts, and as such, I got the grand tour (which I loved, by the way!). One of the many congregations we visited was in the "campo" (or, as we say in the South, "in the sticks"). This country congregation had a meeting room for worship that was attached to the pastor's house. I remember vividly walking through the pastor's cement floor living room, through the kitchen where someone was cooking rice and beans, and into the sanctuary. The room where the believers gathered many times a week for worship was considerably smaller than the coffee shop I am sitting in right now as I type. The floors were cement. The walls were bare. There were some plastic lawn chairs for seating. And I had a strong sense of the presence of God.

We stood in the sanctuary for a few minutes talking, and as we talked, I looked around and realized that I didn't see any musical instruments whatsoever. Curious, I asked, "When you gather together, what musical instruments do you use to worship God?" The pastor dropped his head, embarrassed. He said, "We sing with our voices." And then he paused, as if he was not sure if

137

he should continue to share or not: "And we sometimes bang on those paint cans over there." I looked, and sure enough, in the corner of the worship space were some paint cans. Ready-made drums. That corner was where the worship band sat and led God's people in worship. I have thought many times about this interaction since it happened. I have thanked God again and again, and sometimes with tears in my eyes, for the believers worshipping him in that place. I have wondered why the pastor was embarrassed. And I think I know. He was probably comparing the music at his church with what he thought the music was like at my church or what he knew the music was like at the church down the street.

At some point, and I believe it is early in life, we learn a terrible technique. We learn to compare ourselves with those around us. We do it often, and many times when we don't realize we are doing it. And it robs us of joy. As worship leaders, we may think:

"I can't sing as high as that guy on the radio, so I must not be a real worship leader."

"We don't have an electric guitar player who can play that solo that is on the recording, so we'd better not do that song."

"Our gospel choir only has one tenor, and we just don't have the power of the choir across town."

"We don't have an organ player at our church. We are missing something."

It is very easy to spend a lot of time and energy thinking about what we don't have. Instead, let us use our valuable time thinking about what we do have; and like those Cuban believers, let us praise God with it wholeheartedly! Do you have someone in your congregation who plays the mandolin? Find a way to be creative and make room for that person to offer his gift with your praise band. Do you have only one Korean at your church (and she doesn't sing a lick)? Maybe she could read scripture or lead in prayer, or even speak a verse of a hymn in Korean while your instruments play. Are all your drummers going on vacation at the same time? Have "Acoustic Guitar Sunday" during which four acoustic players lead worship together.

I am reminded of something that happened to Jesus and his disciples. They were in an intense season of ministry, and there were people everywhere. The disciples noticed that it was getting late in the day and that the people were in need of food. Mark 6 records it this way:

Late in the day, his disciples came to him and said, "This is an isolated place, and it's already late in the day. Send them away so that they can go to the surrounding countryside and villages and buy something to eat for themselves." He replied, "You give them something to eat." But they said to him, "Should we go off and buy bread worth almost eight months' pay and give it to them to eat?" He said to them, "How much bread do you have? Take a look." (Mark 6:35-38)

More than five thousand people are in need of food. The disciples recognize the issue, but they just want it to go away. Instead, Jesus commands them to do something about it. Immediately, they begin thinking about what it would take to fix the problem. And very quickly, they become focused on what they *don't* have. Jesus, with a question, refocuses them. He says essentially, "What *do* you have?" "Find out." "Focus your energy there." They do as he says and realize that they have a little boy's lunch. Some bread and some fish. And in the hands of Jesus, that became enough. In fact, it became more than enough.

Scripture also records that when Gideon is arguing with God about why he can't do what God has told him he will do, God says in Judges 6:14, "Go in the strength you have and save Israel out of Midian's hand. Am I not sending you?" (NIV). In other words, "I am going to work with what you have. And don't forget that you have me on your side." That sounds like freedom to me. Similarly, when Moses is wondering what kind of opposition he will face when he does what God has told him to do, God asks him a question: "What is that in your hand?" Moses looks and sees a simple, ordinary staff that is so familiar it has almost become a part of him. Nothing special. Nothing miraculous. "A staff," he replies. And in no time, because of God's extraordinary power, that staff becomes a miraculous tool. With the staff of God (notice this change of terms in Exodus 4:20), Moses turns water into blood and dust into gnats. With Moses's staff, God parts the Red Sea and provides water in the desert. And so, I ask you, what is in your hand? And how might God be able to use that in the ministry he has given you?

Think Creatively

As you reflect on who and what God has given you, give yourself freedom to think outside the box. The best multicultural worship leaders lead creatively. Who says that you can't play that gospel song with an acoustic guitar? Who says that you can't sing a song a cappella during the worship service? Who says that a Korean classical pianist and an African drummer can't play together on the same song? Recently, at Nikki's church, a multicultural choir sang in English and sign language while a Black gospel pianist played with a violist and a Dobro player. Here's a little more about that.

[Nikki] Our choir sings once a month at Bridgeway. While many churches around the country are doing away with their choirs due to a perception that a large choir is irrelevant and screams of traditions that some would rather run from, we utilize our choir strategically at our church. A choir full of people representing a plethora of varying cultures and ethnicities is a powerful visual of the creativity and harmony of the heart of our God.

> A choir full of people representing a plethora of varying cultures and ethnicities is a powerful visual of the creativity and harmony of the heart of our God.

On this particular Sunday, our initial plan was to have the choir sing with just a grand piano (the choir will oftentimes sing along with a full band). Given that the piano player for the day has a background in Black gospel, jazz, and R & B and that I would be the one leading worship that day, I knew that our musical sound could very well be perceived as appealing to one cultural group alone. So, we asked ourselves the question, how can we diversify this sound and include more diverse people in the process and planning?

We made the decision to bring in one of our instrumentalists who is a Dobro player. Don't know what it is? Look it up on YouTube. Essentially, it is an instrument primarily associated with bluegrass music. We also decided that this would be a good time to add a viola player. Not only did this diversify our sound, but also it allowed us to include one of our seventeen-year-old students in the process. That week our choir also learned ASL (American Sign Language) to the chorus of a familiar song. We were able to teach our congregation the ASL for the word *King* and also affirm and speak to our Deaf population at our church.

We created a sound that we had not yet heard before at our church. A choir singing rock music, accompanied by a Black jazz piano player, a Caucasian Dobro player, and a young viola player. It was a wonderful way to include an array of ethnicities, cultures, and ages!

[Josh] Notice that Nikki did not say to the Dobro player, "I am sorry. Your instrument doesn't fit in our sound. You will have to go somewhere else if you want to play your instrument in worship." She did not say, "The church down the street doesn't use the Dobro, so we won't either." She did not say, "There are no Dobros on the radio version of these songs, so we don't need one." Instead, she recognized the value and the beauty and the uniqueness of someone God has placed in her congregation. She gave him an opportunity to use his gifts to benefit others. She affirmed that there are special ways that he was created and can be creative to reflect God's glory.

Reflect

Take some time to make a long list of what and who you do have in your worship ministry. Maybe, like the disciples, you will have to go and look. Find out. Talk to people. Lean into the awkwardness. Brainstorm with others. Conduct a survey. Take the posture of a learner. Be sure you don't overlook the most ordinary of things (like Moses's staff). And don't forget the Lord's presence and call as your greatest resource. Here are some categories of things to get you started:

1. What *instruments/instrumentalists* do you have in your congregation?

2. What kinds of *vocalists* do you have in your congregation?

3. What *languages* do people speak in your congregation?

4. What *nonmusical art forms* are represented in your congregation (dance, photography, painting, drawing, drama, mime, quilting, fashion design, graphic design, carpentry, pottery, sculpture, culinary arts, and so on)?

Embracing God's Glory in Different Cultures

The truth is that God has deposited distinct reflections of his glory into the different people and cultures of our world. In each culture there are things that honor God and line up with God's truth and character. (In each culture there are things that are in contradiction to God's truth and character as well, but that is for another book.) I (Josh) have learned so much from my brothers and sisters in Christ from all around the world. When I look at the way my Eastern Asian friends honor their elders, I see the glory of God built into that culture. When I see and hear how my South Sudanese brothers and sisters are rejoicing in the Lord, even in the midst of great tribulation, I see God getting glory. When I see my Latin American brothers and sisters taking care of their family, even far extended family, I see a glimpse of the glory of God. I see God's glory in the passion and intensity of Brazilians, in the perseverance of Koreans, and in the enthusiasm and zest for life of Jamaicans. We have such an incredible opportunity to learn from one another.

When I look at the way my Eastern Asian friends honor their elders, I see the glory of God built into that culture. When I see and hear how my South Sudanese brothers and sisters are rejoicing in the Lord, even in the midst of great tribulation, I see God getting glory. When I see my Latin American brothers and sisters taking care of their family, even far extended family, I see a glimpse of the glory of God. I see God's glory in the passion and intensity of Brazilians, in the perseverance of Koreans, and in the enthusiasm and zest for life of Jamaicans. We have such an incredible opportunity to learn from one another.

Recently, my family chose to visit a mostly Nigerian congregation on a Sunday morning. I had met one of their members, Isaac, in passing the week before. When I found out he was Nigerian, I asked him if he speaks Yoruba. He was surprised I knew of his language and even more surprised that I could sing songs to praise God in his language. One of the songs was familiar to him, and he readily sang along. We had a neat connection in the Lord in someone's driveway, at a garage sale, believe it or not! He invited me to his church, and a week or two later, I accepted his invitation and took my wife and four blonde kids to his church. From the moment we walked in the door, it was obvious from our skin color that we were visitors. And we were amazed at how welcome they made us feel! Their gift of hospitality far exceeded anything we had experienced before. Someone met us at the door and escorted us to prime seats toward the front. They mentioned that they dressed down as a church that day, to help us feel more welcome. (That was thoughtful, as my wife doesn't own any African outfits! My wardrobe is a little more eclectic, but still.) They recognized us during the service and greeted us warmly. They even sang us a welcome song. They gave us gift bags with books and snacks. Afterward, they gave us a traditional Nigerian delicacy and explained it to us. They also fed us cake and ice cream. They remembered our names and called us by name as we walked through the halls. They introduced us to others in the congregation. One man even got his wife out of a meeting to meet us. They walked us to our vehicle at the end and waved as we left. Later that evening, two different people contacted us—one by text and the other by phone—simply to say how glad they were that we had joined them. A few days later, my family reflected on what they had done to make us feel welcome. And we talked specifically about what we could learn from their example.

Opportunities like this abound in a multicultural church setting. But they don't just *happen* very often. I realize as I look back on this interaction that, first of all, I had learned about Nigerian culture and language a bit from other friends as I have had opportunity. My knowledge of praise songs in Yoruba provided an open door to more conversation and helped us realize that we both love and worship Jesus. Once we realized this connection, my friend Isaac extended an invitation into his world, his church. I could have just received it as a nicety and forgotten about it. Instead, I accepted and brought some of my world (my family!) with me to share with Isaac and his church family. Later, my family was intentional to take time to reflect and talk with one another about our experiences, and we took a posture of learners. At any point in this process, something could have broken down, and we would have missed the benefit of this experience. At any point in this process, Isaac or I could have leaned away from the awkwardness, and we would have forfeited something extremely valuable.

Reflect

What can you learn from the people from different cultures that God has placed around you?

What might you need to do to lean *into* the awkwardness instead of *away* from it?

Turn Challenges into Assets

As you reflect on who and what God has given you, don't only think about the *positive* things. The obstacles and challenges you face could actually be turned into something beneficial. Didn't God promise that he works all things for good for those who love him and are called according to his purpose? Doesn't *all* things include the challenges and the obstacles? Do you believe this? In this Romans 8 passage, the purpose God has called us to is clearly stated. God desires to make us more and more into the image of Christ. And there is absolutely *nothing* that comes into your life, no matter how bad, that God can't use to make you look more like Jesus. That's the long-term benefit. It is sure. God has promised. But there can be benefits in the short term as well. Let me share a story with you.

The obstacles and challenges you face could actually be turned into something beneficial.

I (Josh) remember a time when I was teaching some young worshippers a beginning piano class. We had more people show up than we expected (a good problem to have!) and the room was full. We had eleven students from five different cultures and only five pianos. Of the five pianos, one had dysfunctional keys and one didn't work at all. I was tempted to focus on what I didn't have in that moment. I was tempted to think that the Lord hadn't given us everything we needed. I was tempted to be frustrated and discouraged before I even started to teach these eager worshippers. Instead, by the grace of God, I saw an opportunity. One of the values of our ministry is cross-cultural relationship. And here we were in a tiny room with people from five different cultures! I decided to partner students up on the keyboards and have them work together and interact with one another as they learned. It was beautiful to see a Hispanic boy and an African American girl working together on finger numbers. It warmed my heart to see a Bosnian teenager letting a little White American girl sit on her lap so they could learn together. Quite honestly, had each student had his or her own keyboard, we would have missed this opportunity for interaction. The end result was better because the obstacle was turned into an asset.

I realize that something really wonderful would have been missed if I had chosen to focus on what we didn't have. Yet, that is so easy to do. Oftentimes, we can focus on what we don't have, and as a result, we never start anything. We are not prepared enough. We are not resourced enough. We don't have the right degree. Please, don't give in to the temptation toward discouragement. Trust that God has given and will give you everything you need for your situation (2 Pet 1:3). Trust that he works all things together for good for his people! Ask for his perspective on the challenges you face. Be willing to surrender your plan in order to see what he might want to do in your situation. Remember that multicultural worship is God's desire, and he is working toward it more than we ever will! And make the choice to worship him with whatever is in your hand, no matter how challenging or insignificant it might seem. He is worth it!

Reflect

(This is a good exercise for your worship team or staff team. Having a diverse group work together on this will be beneficial, as some will be more quickly able to identify the challenges and others will be more prone to come up with solutions.)

Divide a sheet of paper into three columns. In the first column, list all the challenges and obstacles that are keeping you from your goal of multicultural worship on earth as it in heaven. Then, take a few minutes to brainstorm potential solutions to these problems. List those in the second column. Now, assume that none of the problems in the first column could ever be solved. Take some time to consider how these problems could be turned into an asset or an opportunity! Write those possibilities in the third column.

Chapter 13
Beyond the Songs

Multicultural worship is more than simply singing songs in different languages. Every element in the service is an opportunity to speak someone's language and connect with someone's heart.

Worship is not just music. We have heard this before. And still we struggle to think clearly about this issue. Often, the language we use doesn't help. (As we will see in chapter 15, language can frame the way we think.) We call people "worship leaders" but then only allow them to lead the music in the service. We call the time of singing before a sermon the "worship time" and clearly distinguish between worship and preaching. One of the passages of scripture that consistently challenges me is Romans 12:1-2: "So, brothers and sisters, because of God's mercies, I encourage you to present your bodies as a living sacrifice that is holy and pleasing to God. This is your appropriate priestly service. Don't be conformed to the patterns of this world, but be transformed by the renewing of your minds so that you can figure out what God's will is—what is good and pleasing and mature."

Worship is not just music.

Clearly, from a biblical standpoint, worship is much more than just singing. That said, the most frequent command in scripture is to sing. Music is powerful and important, and God has ordained it for his praise. So, let's consider for a few moments some creative ways to use music in multicultural worship.

Worship Does Not Equal Music

Employ Song Medleys

Take a song from one culture and connect it with a song from another culture. If done well, this can communicate that these songs (and consequently the people from the cultures they represent) belong together and work well together. When creating song medleys, consider carefully the musical connection. It helps if both songs can be sung in the same key comfortably, if the tempo can remain steady throughout the medley, and if the styles have some points of connection. As carefully as you consider the musical connecting points, consider the themes of the songs. Are there concepts in the two songs that connect with each other? If so, connect the songs at that point if at all possible. Maybe the chorus of one song shares a similar idea to the bridge of another song. Then, move from the bridge of the one song into the chorus of the other. This will help the congregation feel a stronger connection between the two songs. We like to sing a Congolese song called "Yesu Azali Awa" in the language of Lingala. The chorus is simple and very accessible for non-Lingala speakers, and the words literally mean "Jesus is here with us." I like to lead this song and then go right into singing the old hymn, "I stand amazed in the presence of Jesus the Nazarene."[1] The tempos and keys match, and the concepts connect so it just makes sense to go from one into the other.

Change the Style of a Familiar Song

Why not sing "What a Friend We Have in Jesus" with simple African percussion and vocals? Even though we might not sing any African songs or languages, this is a good way to engage African heart music and culture. Tastefully adding a sitar or a didgeridoo to a song can have many positive effects, as we mentioned in chapter 11.

Engage Different Languages in the Same Song

Sing the first verse in English and the second verse in Spanish. Sing the same bridge a few times in a row in a different language each time. Have one person on your worship team sing the chorus of a song in English while another harmonizes with her in Swahili. Put multiple languages on the screen

---

1. Charles H. Gabriel, "I Stand Amazed in the Presence," 1905.

even if you are not singing them from the stage. Additionally, a new kind of worship song is being written that can't be sung in one language only but must be sung in two or more languages back and forth. We will go into much more detail on engaging language in the next chapter.

Leverage Background Music

Choose strategically the music you have playing when people enter the worship space. If you want to honor a particular culture but don't have them represented in the worship service that Sunday, why not play some worship music in their style/language as people are walking in? Maybe your dance team could dance to a song in Korean. Or maybe the video you make of photos from your Vacation Bible School could have a song in French as the background. Don't underestimate the power of even seemingly small things.

More Than a Song

As we stated above, worship is more than simply music. Every element in the service is an opportunity to speak someone's language and connect with his or her heart.

Visual Images Set the Scene

What adorns the walls of the hallways that people travel on their way to the sanctuary? Are there pictures of diverse people in your lobby? Do you have any visual portrayals of Jesus? If so, what color/ethnicity is he? What might that communicate? Is that what you want to communicate? What background images do you use on your screen? Woven palm fronds or color-ful cloth can evoke feelings of someone's home country. Even background images can help people feel considered. If you have multiple languages on your screen, is English always on top? What might this communicate? Are words in other languages spelled correctly and with the appropriate accent marks?

Offering

As I (Josh) mentioned earlier, my family and I worship in a different cultural context every week. I have been in churches where they don't mention the offering, but simply have a box in the back for people to give if they wish. I have been in other churches where the offering plates are passed around again if not enough is gathered the first time. I have been in churches where we danced the offering forward to a box. Some churches pass offering plates. Others pass baskets. Once, I was in a church that emptied out some ladies purses and passed those. If there are ushers in your church, who are they? Could children collect the offering? Could people from different cultures/ages/generations work together to collect the offering? What might this communicate?

Preaching

In different cultures, there are different levels and ways of interacting with the preacher (remember *power distance* from chapter 6?). In some cultures, if the congregation is quiet, it is a sign of respect. In other cultures, if the congregation is quiet, it is a sign of disengagement. It may be important for both of these to be present on some level in your multicultural congregation. Additionally, the stories and illustrations used in a sermon should be considered carefully as they will affect different cultures differently. (Note: Psalm 19 has an interesting commentary: "Heaven is declaring God's glory." It goes on to say that its sound "extends throughout the world" and reaches "the ends of the earth." Nature is something that's common to all of us. So, when you can use illustrations from nature, that's going to relate to a lot more people than illustrations from insider culture things.) Or, if you're going to use an illustration that is inside to one culture, then explain what it means. Lastly, sermon *length* is cultural. In some contexts, if a sermon goes for thirty minutes it is too long. In others, the preacher has just finished his introduction after thirty minutes. It may be good for sermon length to vary from week to week in a multicultural church.

Mime

Some art forms, such as mime, require no language whatsoever. There is something very human about mime. This can be especially effective in a multicultural worship community. Please know, however, that you must be careful introducing nonverbal ways of communicating. Not every culture will interpret things the same way. You need to try them out. I once heard of a group who introduced mime to a culture not their own, and the costumes and painted faces conjured up images of pagan worship in their audience. Just like music is *not* a universal language (a song I think sounds "happy" might not be "happy" to you), your art forms may not appeal to everyone the same way.

Dance

Dance is also a nonverbal art form. It may be a welcome change for people to simply listen to an instrumental piece of music and watch as dancers lead their hearts in worship. To have space in a worship service where there are no words is especially helpful to people who are working hard to understand the main language of the service. This gives their brains a break!

Painting/Drawing

You may have talented visual artists in your community who could illustrate what is being preached or sung about during any given service. These visuals can really appeal to the visual learners in your congregation, and they can serve as a long-lasting memorial of what is communicated.

Video

Proskuneo created a multilingual video of the Lord's Prayer. We had some of our friends who speak different languages come into a studio and read the Lord's Prayer in their language and also in English. Then, we pasted the audio of those together in a creative way and added the written language in white on a plain black screen. Simple! But imagine your heart language is Haitian Creole and you are sitting in a service that is predominantly in English. Nothing has been sung or spoken in Creole. And then, this video is played, and for a few minutes, you hear your language, and your heart connects with it in a deep way.

Scripture

Scripture can be read by different people in different languages (either live or pre-recorded). Scripture can be on the screen in different languages whether or not those languages are voiced aloud. In some cultures, it is important for the congregation to all stand when the Bible is read. In other cultures, they are accustomed to reading scripture antiphonally. This is a relatively easy way of engaging nonartistic people in leadership during your services.

Prayer

It is also relatively easy to have people lead prayer in different languages. You can choose to have this translated or not. After all, God understands! Or, you could allow people to pray out loud all at once, in their various languages.

Truly, God is big enough to discern all the prayers at once. Or, you could simply lead in a time of silent prayer. In those moments, people are able to pray in their own language, and it may be the one time in the whole service in which they don't have to be translating things in their heads.

Greeting

Throughout the Bible, we read that greetings were important. They are also very cultural. It was really strange as a thirteen-year-old boy to go to my first youth group meeting in a Latin American country. I didn't know what was going to happen, and I was sitting right inside the door, so every girl who walked in the meeting kissed me. Kisses and hugs can communicate the family bond that we share in Jesus. Bowing as a greeting can communicate honor and respect. Greeting time can also be a natural time to teach a phrase of greeting in a different language and allow people to practice it on one another.

These are just a few ideas that we hope will prime the pump of your creativity. This is in no way meant to be an exhaustive list. You have many wonderful opportunities to try new things. In many ways, each time you plan a service you are starting with a blank canvas. Be the creative person that God has made you to be. As your congregation changes and becomes more diverse, it is only appropriate that you try new expressions of worship to God. Be creative! And create in community! Remember, no one person is diverse in himself. It is impractical for one person to plan a multicultural worship service by himself. We need different perspectives and ideas to inform our corporate worship times together.

Reflect

Get to know your congregation. How do they respond to certain things? How did they do things in their churches growing up? What is meaningful to them? What is offensive to them? What part of the worship service do they most connect with?

Relationships are important. Connect what is done in the worship service to people (in, around, and connected to the congregation). Don't simply aim to create worship experiences, but rather develop a worshipping community!

What is one element of a worship service that you can take steps to diversify in your congregation in the next month?

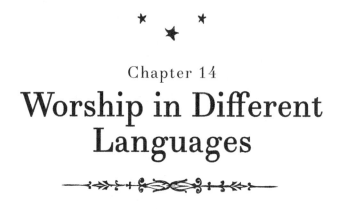

Chapter 14
Worship in Different Languages

*Don't underestimate the power of language. Here's a step-by-step process
for introducing multiple languages in worship.*

In Genesis 12, God used language to separate people so that they would
do what he commanded them to do: spread out over all the earth. In Acts 2,
we see the exact opposite happening, as God uses language to bring people
together when the Holy Spirit is given. Language is powerful. It has the potential to unite and to divide. To inspire and to discourage. To wound and
to heal. It speaks to the deep places inside us, to our hearts. Language is extremely important.

Our heart language is often the way in which we frame our thoughts.

Our heart language is often the way in which we frame our thoughts. If
you have never learned another language, you may not have considered this
reality. The language we use both *reveals* and *clarifies* the way we think about
things. For example, in Korean culture, respect for elders is built into their
language. Quickly after meeting someone, you must ascertain whether that
person is older than you, younger than you, or your same age. If he is older
than you, you must put a different ending on some of your words to communicate respect. The Arabic language distinguishes clearly between male

and female. When I (Josh) say, "How are you?" to Fadi (a male teacher from Syria), it is different than when I ask Raheal (a female Sudanese student), "How are you?" I have to use the correct gender-specific ending so I don't offend. The Spanish language has both the gender and the respect element present in it. It also has another element that I find fascinating. In Spanish, instead of saying, "I dropped the baseball," I would say, "The baseball itself fell from me." Instead of saying, "I lost my keys," I would say, "My keys lost themselves to me." This frames the way I think. Is it my fault that the keys got lost? Or is it the keys' fault? Who is responsible? The Amondawa people of Brazil do not have words to break down time into weeks and years. Instead they think in terms of day and night and rainy and dry seasons. Interesting, no one in their group has an age. Rather, their names change to reflect the stage of life that they are in. For example, when a new baby is born into a family, the older sibling will give up his name to the newborn and will assume a new name. Additionally, cultures will have more words for things that they know very well or highly value. For example, in English, we have one word for *banana*. But there are many kinds of bananas (maybe you didn't know this!). In some tropical countries I have been to, there are many words to distinguish the different kinds of bananas. These kinds of distinctions are not only points of interest but also windows into how a people think and what they value. If you learn even a little bit of someone's language, you have an opportunity to understand that person better. *When you speak someone's heart language, it communicates that you value that person.*

Recently, I took a trip to South Korea to lead worship, teach, and preach. Before I went, I spent a little time learning some basics of the Korean language. I wanted to learn how to introduce myself and say a few basic polite phrases. I also worked hard to memorize a paragraph that I could speak in Korean at the beginning of each one of my talks. It was challenging to memorize something that sounded completely foreign to me. I had Skype sessions with a tutor. I wrote it and rewrote it. I came up with my own phonetic spellings with accent marks to show me where the stresses were on the words. I spoke it over and over again in my car while driving. I felt pretty good about it when I arrived in Korea. But, then, the first chance I had to speak it in front of a group in South Korea, I stumbled all over it. Mispronunciations. Stresses on the wrong syllables. Halting speech. You name it, I did it. To make matters worse, someone in the audience was filming. A week or so later when I saw that someone had posted the video on Facebook, I was dismayed. I had gotten more comfortable with the introduction by then and was able to deliver it much more smoothly. I was embarrassed by how bad I sounded. I was curious to know what the person wrote as an introduction to the video. It was all in Korean, and I had no idea what it said. I assumed it said something like, "Nice try! But not quite." At least that is what I would have said if I had introduced the video. I summoned all my bravery and asked my friend to translate the caption on the video for me. The caption says, "This is what love looks like." I still get tears in my eyes just thinking about it. My heart was to value people by learning their language. And, even in all my mispronunciations and stumbling speech, love came through.

One good question to ask is, "What language do you speak at home?"

It is important to note that even if someone is fluent in a language, it may not be a "heart language" for him. One good question to ask is, "What language do you speak at home?" Oftentimes, this is a significant indicator of heart language. Recently, we held a worship camp for students at our Proskuneo School of the Arts. The entire camp was in English. But when we surveyed our students, 80 percent of them spoke a language other than English at home. This was our clue that though they might be able to learn things cognitively in English, another language might affect their hearts more quickly and profoundly. We decided to memorize Scripture each day in a variety of different languages because we wanted our students to hide God's words in their hearts. Don't just assume that because people in your congregation understand English that it affects their hearts in the same way it affects yours. And don't just assume that because everyone in your congregation understands English, you should always worship together in English. If English is someone's second, third, or fourth language, please know that it likely requires more energy and effort for her to process the entire service in English. Her brain is working overtime, which makes it more difficult for her heart to engage.

Don't just assume that because everyone in your congregation understands English, you should always worship together in English.

> ### Reflect
>
> Conduct a survey (either formally or informally) to find out what languages people in your congregation speak.
>
> Ask them what they like/appreciate about their language. Ask them to teach you a word or phrase in their language. Find a way to record it, practice it, and then use it in conversation with them later.
>
> Find out what languages are represented in your church's neighborhood. This might require a Google search of local businesses as well as walking around the neighborhood. We would encourage both!
>
> Is there a difference between the languages spoken in the neighborhood and the languages spoken by people in your church? Why or why not? What do you think?

So, God has brought people with different heart languages to your congregation and your church's neighborhood? And you want to engage their heart languages during your worship times? We are glad you are motivated. But we want you to be careful in how you go about this. You can actually do more damage than good, if you are not careful. Here are some helpful principles we have learned from experience.

Address the *Why* and the *How* as Well as the *What*

Rather than just jumping right in to the new song in the new language, take a minute or two to help the congregation understand why we are choosing to sing in a different language. Many in your congregation may be asking the question why consciously or even subconsciously. Here are a number of simple explanations as to why:

> # Take a minute or two to help the congregation understand why we are choosing to sing in a different language.

1. "The Bible says that one day, we will be worshipping around the throne with people from every tribe and language. Let's prepare our hearts for that today by singing this next song in *Ki-Swahili*."

2. "There are a number of people in our congregation whose heart language is *Korean*. Let's learn a few phrases in Korean so that we can worship along with them in their heart language this morning!"

3. "Right across the street from our church live many people who speak *Spanish*. This morning as we sing this song in Spanish, let's pray for them and ask God for ways to help us connect with them for his glory!"

4. "God's heart is full of love for all the people of the world. This morning, let's step outside our comfort zone and sing in *Hindi*, asking God to expand our heart for the world around us."

Not only is the *why* important, but so is the *how!* It is wise, before asking the congregation to sing anything in another language, to spend a minute teaching them the pronunciation for some of the key words. It is especially helpful (and empowers diverse leadership) to have a native speaker pronounce a word or short phrase slowly and then have the congregation repeat it back. This way they have a chance to get a handle on the pronunciation before combining it with rhythm and melody.

> # Have a native speaker pronounce a word or short phrase slowly and then have the congregation repeat it back.

Release the Pressure

When you are learning a new language (or new languages), you will make mistakes. It comes with the territory and is part of how God uses language-learning to humble us (which is a good thing). I (Josh) can remember going up to an ice cream counter in Costa Rica and asking for a knife instead of a spoon with which to eat my ice cream. I was met with an amused stare. Then there was the time that a Chin Burmese student was teaching me a song in his language, and I evidently kept pronouncing the word for "Wow, what a nice-looking woman!" instead of the worshipful words I was trying to sing.

People don't like to make mistakes. And people can feel silly making sounds they have never made before. In fact, it can cause them not to want to even try. They would rather sit quietly and protect their reputation than risk making a fool out of themselves. As worship leaders, when we are asking our congregation to take a risk by singing in a language that is unfamiliar, we can do and say a few simple things to release the pressure and help them be more willing to give it a try.

Acknowledge that it is uncomfortable. You could say, "I know this might be uncomfortable for you, but be encouraged . . . God exists outside our comfort zones!" Or, you might say, "Let's try that again to try to get our mouths wrapped around those words a bit better." Don't let the elephant in the room go unaddressed!

Help the congregation have healthy expectations of themselves. Say: "Don't worry if you don't get it right the first time. You should have heard us in practice this week." Or, "If you are having a hard time with all these words, maybe just pick one that gets repeated and try to get that one right!" Or, "Just do your best! God is listening to our hearts this morning as we worship!"

Learn with the congregation. There have been many times that I didn't have the pronunciation down before the service. I have even called people up during a service and asked them to teach me and the congregation the pronunciation for the next song. In those instances, the congregation sees me as a leader learning along with them and making mistakes, and that releases the pressure tremendously.

Don't Give Up Too Soon

First of all, anyone who has ever learned another language will tell you that this does not happen overnight. It can take weeks or months before you even learn how to pronounce certain unique sounds correctly. And in any given congregation, there will be people who are good at picking up other languages and people for whom it will be incredibly difficult.

Second, remember that there is a discrepancy between how much time you spend listening to the song, picking out the song, and learning it to teach to your praise team and how much time the praise team gets to learn the song during rehearsal. And there is an even greater discrepancy (most likely) between the amount of time the praise team gets to work on a song in a new language during rehearsal and the five minutes that the congregation gets during the service. It may be months before a congregation really *gets* a song. It is worth all the hard work if a song becomes part of a congregation's DNA. Let me give you a beautiful example from my own family.

I (Josh) am reminded of the time that my four-year-old daughter, Miriam, went with me to a Sudanese church. All the songs were in Arabic, and some with Swahili as well. And one, "Mighty to Save," was in English. After the service, Miriam said she didn't know most of the songs but was happy that one was in English. When I questioned her, she said the English song was "Baba Al Fi Sama"—actually, the song was in Arabic. But she has grown up singing that song, and it is her favorite song. So, because it was so familiar and she "gets" it, her little brain decided that must mean it was in English.

Tip: Choose wisely the songs you want to introduce because you will need to stick with them and be dedicated to them if they are to become part of your congregation's worship DNA. Consistency is key! If you go for six months without singing a certain song in a different language, it might feel like relearning it when you bring it back.

Start Small and Go Slowly

When babies are learning language, we get excited about the smallest things. Saying *mama* seems like a huge accomplishment, and it is! It is no different in our congregations. In fact, in many ways, it is more difficult for adults to learn a new language. So, let's start small!

Can You Say Igwe?

Sure you can! That's easy. Say it with me: ihg-weh. Way to go! This is how we introduced the song titled "Igwe" to our congregation. Incorporating languages is still relatively new at Bridgeway Community Church where

I (Nikki) lead worship. My friend Dola, who sings in our choir at church, sent me this fun and joyful song in the African languages of Igbo and Yoruba to introduce to our congregation. The original recorded version of this song has about three different sections to the song. It included a first verse that is entirely in Yoruba, an easy chorus containing one word, and a complicated bridge section sung in a mix of English and Igbo. When I first heard the song, I thought that it may be a bit challenging for our congregation of mostly English-speakers to learn. Particularly since there was so much language to learn. The chorus of the song repeats the word *Igwe* over and over again, which means "King." I knew that this word for Jesus in another language would be a great language-learning on-ramp for the congregation and would keep them engaged and focused during the time of worship and singing without having to spend several minutes learning an entire song in a new language.

My friend Dola led the song that day. Not only did she ease the congregation in with pronouncing the name *Igwe*, but also we explained what language we would be singing and why this was an important song in her Nigerian culture. We were not just singing a song in a different language to be cool or different for the sake of being different. We were connecting this experience to someone right in our community. Our people were thrilled to learn this song, and it was such a fun time of worship and connection. Dola sang the verses, and the congregation joined in after each verse and sang "Igwe." That is all that the congregation had to learn for that song. We made it so that there was an easy and nonthreatening way to include everyone in the room during that moment of worship. Our church loves that song these days, and we have never taught them more than that one phrase.

Here are some effective tactics for introducing new languages in worship music:

1. *Have the lyrics for a song in a different language on the screen, even if you do not sing in that language.*

For example, take the hymn "Amazing Grace." You can find that hymn in Afrikaans, Creole, German, Spanish, Indonesian, Navajo, Portuguese, Russian, and Korean, to name a few languages. If you know people who speak that language and will be in your service, why not put that language on the screen with the English? That way, they could sing along in their heart language or at least read the words in their own language.

I (Josh) was once asked to lead worship for a denominational gathering of multiple churches in a region. I was intentional to choose congregational songs that could be sung in the languages of the churches that would be participating in this gathering, namely, English, Spanish, and Korean. I created PowerPoint slides for these songs and sent them ahead. The night of the event, I arrived for rehearsal and was informed that my PowerPoints were not going to be used. Instead they were going to use the program they normally used, so they could have moving backgrounds. This program would not show different languages in different colors or fonts on the same slide, and so, as a result, they eliminated the Spanish and Korean from the slides. I watched my Korean brothers and sisters try (unsuccessfully) to sing along with the songs in English. After a while, they stopped trying. I was distraught. This church *said* they wanted to be welcoming to people from different countries. But their actions spoke very loudly. They showed by their actions that moving backgrounds were more important than their brothers and sisters participating in their heart languages.

2. *Take a short section (even one word) of a familiar song and sing it in a different language.*

A great example of this is the song "Open the Eyes of my Heart." The bridge section is easy, repeating the words, "Holy, holy, holy," over and over again.[1] This can be an easy first step into language, as you are simply repeating one word like *Santo* ("Holy" in Spanish) over and over again.

3. *Create a medley with a traditional hymn and a global song in a different language.*

One of the benefits to this is that it connects the new with the familiar. Additionally, it shows the congregation that these things are not separate but equal and work well together. A powerful message.

4. *Sing a call-response song.*

The leader sings a line in a different language, and then the congregation echoes. The beauty of this is that you can listen first and then simply

---

1. Paul Baloche, "Open the Eyes of My Heart," Integrity's Hosanna! Music, 1997.

sing what you hear. If the phrases are short, this is also a good first step into language. Much of language is learned by simply mimicking what you hear.

5. *Sing a chorus simultaneously in a bunch of different languages.*

Everyone picks a different language and sings the chorus simultaneous and multilingually. The benefit to this is that no one is left out or waiting for the chance to sing their language. We are all actively engaging in our own language at the same time.

6. *American Sign Language adds a different language on top of the sung English.*

It can be a very beautiful expression (as with any language, you have to be careful that the song is well-interpreted) and can add a visual expression for those in your congregation who are more visually oriented.

7. *Sing an entire verse of a song in one language.*

Then go back and sing the verse in a different language. Not everyone on the praise team needs to know the other language. You only need one strong singer to lead out.

You may, in fact, dwell for a while on each of these steps with your congregation. It might take a few months of having different languages on the screen before they are ready to begin singing a song in a different language. Also, *please* reiterate songs and languages that you teach. Once you take the time to teach a phrase, chorus, or song in a different language, find ways to work that in to the services over the next few weeks and months. In doing so, you are helping the congregation add this to their worship repertoire. And after a while, instead of thinking of it as "a song for those people," they may very well think of it as "our song."

Reiterate songs and languages that you teach.

Integrate Languages into the Entire Service

If we are not careful, and if languages only appear at times in songs and nowhere else in the service, we communicate the message that we do not fully affirm and embrace different languages as an integral part of our church. They can exist here in this little area but nowhere else. This message, though often unintentional, can be detrimental.

In the last chapter, we went into detail as to how to make the different nonmusical service elements multicultural in expression. Here are a few reminders of how multiple languages can be engaged in these elements.

1. Have the word *Welcome* on your screen or in your bulletin in different languages.

2. During greeting time, teach a short phrase in a different language that can be used for saying "Hello!"

3. Pastors can use words in different languages for illustrations in their sermons.

4. Scripture can be read in different languages.

5. Prayers can be prayed in different languages.

Make It Personal

When my daughter Miriam was just two years old, she was just barely getting a hold on English. She had just recently started making complete sentences. She said the word *me* in place of *my, mine,* and *I.* So clearly, language was not her forte. Because of our family's deep cross-cultural relationships, however, she had a crash course in Spanish. A longtime friend from the Dominican Republic and his wife and daughter came to stay at our house for a week. Their daughter, Beatriz, was Miriam's instant friend. Only, Beatriz knew no English. And Miriam knew no Spanish. They played together well all week despite the language barrier. In fact, I wasn't sure whether or not Miriam even noticed the language difference until about a month after our Spanish-speaking friends left. I made a phone call to a local Hispanic pastor and left him a voicemail in Spanish. Miriam watched and listened while I talked. At the end of the call she said, "Are you talking to Beatriz?" To her, what she heard wasn't Spanish; it was the language Beatriz speaks. When Miriam heard it, she immediately thought of her friend.

This is a huge lesson for us in the church. Rather than thinking of ourselves and spouting out things like, "That's not my style of music," or, "Do we have to sing in Mexican again?" (yes, I have heard that before), what if we were to think about others in our congregation and in the global body of Christ?

As worship leaders, we can help people make it personal. We must work to connect what we do in worship to our relationships. Here are a few ideas:

1. Have someone from your congregation who speaks the "other" language introduce the song. That person could also teach the pronunciation. After all, he is the expert in that regard! The congregation will connect the language with the person who introduced it.

2. On a day that you pray for a missionary to a certain country or send a missions team out to a certain country or listen to a report from a returning mission team from a certain country, sing a song in the language of that country.

3. As you are introducing a song in worship, name-drop in a way that communicates honor and promotes relationship. For example, "The other day as our brother Abraham [maybe even point him out in the congregation, if this is appropriate] and I were eating dinner together, I asked him if he had any songs that he sang in church back in the Sudan that were especially meaningful to him. His eyes lit up, and he taught me this song. I am so excited to be able to share it with you."

Singing with Emnet

My friend Emnet is from Ethiopia and speaks the native language of Amharic. Emnet also works on staff with me (Nikki) at Bridgeway. Emnet has a gentle, quiet, and calming spirit as well as a hidden singing talent. One day at the office, I stopped over at Emnet's desk, resting my forearms on the high wood panel. Leaning in close to her I asked, "Do you know any songs in Amharic that you could teach me?" She gave me that "Nikki, what are you up to?" look. To my surprise, she responded, "What type of song are you looking for?" I told her that I was looking for a song to teach to the congregation that was easy to pick up, sing with, and engage in. She told me that she would have something to teach me by the end of the week.

Friday came, and I passed by Emnet's desk again. She'd mentioned to me that she had a song to teach me but that she was nervous to sing it for me because she doesn't consider herself a singer. I assured her that she was safe with me and invited her to come to my office where we could close the door and she could sing it for me. Sitting in my office, Emnet began to teach me a beautiful worship song in Amharic called "Eyesus," which translates into the name *Jesus*. As soon as she began singing it, I knew that our congregation would latch on to it. I recorded Emnet singing the song and speaking the pronunciations so that I could then teach the song to the congregation.

A few months later, our church hosted a Sunday dedicated to the ministry of Compassion International and child sponsorship. One of the countries that our church had begun to focus on was Ethiopia. We have several people from Ethiopia within our congregation, and our leadership thought that it would just make sense to connect with a country that was represented in our midst. As I was going about choosing music for this particular Sunday, I had remembered the beautiful song in Amharic that Emnet had taught me months prior. I went over to Emnet's desk again, forearms on that high wood panel, and, leaning in, I asked, "Emnet, would you be willing to teach our congregation the song, 'Eyesus'?" I thought she was going to faint. You see, Emnet prefers to be in the background serving people instead of being in front of a large group of them. I told her that I would be right there with her on stage, singing with her, and how I thought that it would be so much more influential and powerful if she would sing it and teach it because she is from Ethiopia. After a few hot flashes, some sweat, and some nervous laughter, Emnet agreed to sing and teach the song as well as tell the story of the song and about her own experience as someone coming to this country.

This was probably one of my most memorable and favorite stories in leading multicultural worship. This process of finding a song, learning a song, teaching a song, and connecting a song with a congregation of English-speakers is not always a fast and easy process. But what I do believe is that pursuing Emnet in her own way and her own time was critical for our relationship and doing this with her was just as important for me as the leader as it was for her. Last, providing some additional *context* for a congregation can go a long way in them accepting a song in a language they are not familiar with. "Eyesus" was not just a random song in Amharic to learn but now is forever connected to sweet Emnet, a beautiful woman, who is a part of our community, and who has shared her culture and her world with us all.

Reflect

Are you leveraging language in a way that is engaging people's hearts?

What is a good next step (or first step) for your church in terms of incorporating different languages into worship?

Should We Sing in a Language That No One in Our Congregation Speaks?

I get this question a lot. So, I am glad you asked.

Before you go too much further, are you sure *that no one in your congregation speaks that language?*

Are there really none of those people in your congregation? No one whose heart language is Spanish or Korean? If you were to look at me, you would never guess that Spanish is one of my heart languages. You can't tell by looking at someone what languages she does or does not speak. And if there is even one of those people in your congregation, then truly "them is us," as a good friend of mine likes to say.

You can't tell by looking at someone what languages she does or does not speak.

Here are four good reasons to sing in a language that no one in your congregation speaks:

1. *Because worship is not only expressive, but formative.*

We should sing in worship, not only the things that express our hearts but also the things that *should* express our hearts. (like teaching a kid to say *thank you*, it actually can cultivate thankfulness). If we are only expressive in our worship, we would never sing, "In all I do, I honor You."[1] Because we all know that is just not true. However, it is what we want to be true.

Singing a song in a foreign language can make us more aware of our neighbors across the street or around the world. It can cultivate a heart within us for those who are different from us. It can remind us that God's heart is for the people in the community surrounding our church. And our hearts should be for them as well. If they aren't, we shouldn't be content with that. So, singing a song in one of those languages could be a way in which we put our hearts in position for God to share more of his heart for those people with us. What cultures and languages are spoken right around your church building?

2. Because worship is not about us.

There is a real tendency in us to make worship all about us these days. How many times have you heard, "The band was tight today. They played some of my favorite songs. Worship was awesome today!" If we don't like the worship at one church, we just find another church. As if worship were about pleasing us. Worship is about God and his glory. Is one language adequate for fully expressing God's glory? Is one musical style sufficient? Singing a song in a different language can be an opportunity to see God as bigger than my own language, my own cultural style, my own preferences, my own boxes that I put him in.

3. Because God exists outside my comfort zone.

Many churches have worship wars (or worship skirmishes) over traditional and contemporary, and so they ask, "Why in the world would I add a different language or style to the mix?" The people in your congregation may find that they are on common uncomfortable ground if you sing a song that isn't comfortable for anybody. And in that moment, recognize that God can be honored by our humility, by our teachability, by our willingness to get outside ourselves, by our desire to see him exalted.

4. Because it levels the playing field.

Let's say you are part of a multicultural congregation that has people who speak Spanish, Korean, and English. One Sunday you introduce a song

---

1. Billy J. Foote, "You are My King (Amazing Love)," worshiptogether.com songs, 1996.

in Lingala from the Congo. Before you teach it, you say, "Does anyone here speak Lingala?" No one raises their hand. "Good!" you say. "That means we are all learning this together." All of the sudden, the entire congregation is outside of their comfort zone together. This is brilliant! At other times, when you are singing in Spanish, some people feel great while others struggle. The same thing happens when you sing in Korean and English. But, in this instance, everyone is on level ground. You have common ground in an uncommon language. How about that?

Additional Resources: Proskuneo has a video series entitled "Incorporating Language into Musical Worship" that is available for free on our blog at www .proskuneo.org/blog.

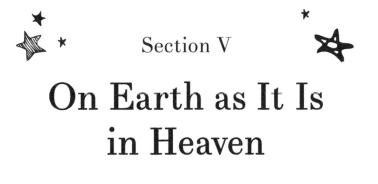

Section V

On Earth as It Is in Heaven

[It's not always easy. But, it's always worth it!]

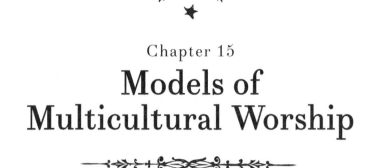

Chapter 15
Models of Multicultural Worship

Here are four basic models of multiethnic worship and the benefits and challenges for each. Which one might be helpful for you?

I (Josh) am soberly aware that there are dangers in presenting and considering models. First of all, let me say that *there is no perfect model for multicultural worship.* All have benefits and challenges (I am resisting the use of the terms *pros* and *cons*). It would be a shame for you to read through this chapter on models, pick the one that seems best to you, and then believe it is the one perfect way to do multicultural worship. Please don't do that.

> # Essentially all models are wrong, but some are useful.
> # —George E. P. Box

Also, there is no way your church can look *exactly* like a model. The other day, my kids and I were talking about the concept of a "normal" day. My son hopes for "perfectly normal" days. As we considered this together for a bit, we realized that there really is no such thing as a "perfectly normal" day, because what we hold to be normal is actually a combination of things that happen on most days. No one day has them all, but most days have most of them. We put all of those together and assume that is a perfectly normal day. An unattainable standard. Please don't look to one of these models as your standard and be frustrated that you never attain it fully.

God is doing *new* things, and we need to respond in *new* ways.

Lastly, these four models are not the *only* four ways that multicultural worship is viable. There may be ways of combining these models to make something that better fits your context. There may be entirely new ideas that have yet to be considered. This is certainly a season in the life of the church in which God is doing *new* things, and we need to respond in *new* ways. These are the four basic models I have seen used in the last eleven years as my life has been devoted to the concept of multicultural worship. I have been in a lot of different churches and conferences and worship services. I have seen, experienced, and considered a lot. And I am trying to distill that information and simplify it in a way that will hopefully be helpful to you.

I hope these models will help you think intentionally. So many times we just react and do what seems natural in the moment. Very few colleges and seminaries are training ministers in multicultural worship competencies. Many multicultural churches have become multicultural by "accident," and they are still operating and worshipping the way they did when they were monocultural churches. Often we are two or three or ten years into ministry and never stop to ask, "Why do we do things this way?" or "Is there a better way?" Please, stop and ask these questions.

I hope these models will demystify things for you a bit. Sometimes the concept of multicultural worship is mysterious. We have never seen it done. We see glimpses of heaven, but there is no order of service listed in Revelation so we don't know how to work it out practically. So many times, I have heard people say, "I believe in the concept of multicultural worship, but I have no idea how to actually do it." Sometimes things seem so mysterious that we don't ever start. If you believe in multicultural worship here on earth, please start. Pick a model and try it.

The concept of multicultural worship is mysterious. We see glimpses of heaven, but there is no order of service listed in Revelation.

As we consider these models, I am going to use the analogy of food and meals. We all eat. We all enjoy some foods and not others. Food is universal. And it seems from the talk about the marriage supper of the Lamb that food is eternal. I have to say I am happy about that! Lastly, food is a cultural phenomenon. What is considered the perfect dessert in one culture doesn't even fit in the category of dessert in another culture.

Exhibit A: 1 Main Dish (rotates) / 1 Side Dish (rotates) Model

Imagine a Sunday dinner plate that has a beautiful Argentinian steak, cooked to perfection. (For some people, that is a meal in itself!) And, then, on the side, a tangy Greek salad with black olives and feta cheese. The next Sunday dinner is a large bowl of chicken and veggie pesto pasta. And, on the side, a skewer of tropical fruits (papaya, pineapple, and mango).

The idea here is that the bulk of the worship service is in one musical style/language/cultural expression. But one special element (maybe an offertory song, special music, call to worship, or some other part) is in a different musical style/language/cultural expression. Now, if there are only two cultures present in your church, this model could work without having to rotate. Just make sure that the cultures take turns being the main dish and the side dish. In a multicultural church (in which more than two cultures are present), however, there is need for more rotation with this model. So, the following Sunday, the bulk of the service is in a different style from the week before, as is the special element.

Let's flesh this out a bit. I have heard my friend Mark DeYmaz who pastors Mosaic Church of Central Arkansas (www.mosaicchurch.net) talk about how they have, at times, employed this model with their congregation. (For more concerning Mark's thoughts related to worship in a multiethnic church see *Leading a Healthy Multi-Ethnic Church: Seven Common Challenges and How to Overcome Them* by Mark DeYmaz and Harry Li [Grand Rapids: Zondervan, 2010], 133-138). I am taking what I have heard from him and filling in some details with my sanctified imagination. The first Sunday of the month, they may have a Christian Contemporary Music (CCM) team leading songs that are well known by younger White American believers. Acoustic and electric guitars work together to build the musical foundation. Then, for the offertory, an Indian man with a sitar plays and sings a *Yesu bhajan*, a devotional song to Jesus, in both English and Hindi. The second Sunday of the month, maybe a Latino team will lead songs in a mixture of English and Spanish. The rhythms are distinctly Latin, and percussion abounds. This Sunday, however, the prayer time is Korean style. A Korean leader in the congregation helps the congregation pray out loud at the same time as many Korean churches are accustomed to. The third Sunday of the month, the service opens with the traditional European hymn, "Holy, Holy, Holy," led by one older White man at a piano. Then, a Black gospel choir leads the extended time of worship. The bulk of the service feels authentically Black gospel. I am picturing an organ, a killer bass/drums combo, and some powerful yet agile vocal harmonies. You get the idea.

I have heard Mark say that this model is much like a family eating dinner together. For one meal, maybe they will have pizza, and the younger members of the family eat with gusto, while Grandma works hard to finish one piece. The next meal, Grandma is excited about the baked potato and green veggies, while the children eat the minimum requirements. In a month, all have had something that they appreciate and enjoy. And, most importantly, they have all been together. When a church engages this model of worship, you might hear them say frequently, "If you didn't get what you like this week, come back next week! It will be totally different."

As with every model, there are some real benefits and real challenges that come with this approach.

Some Benefits

1. People have time to really soak in the kind of music and worship they appreciate. If Black gospel is your heart music, then on Black gospel Sunday you are in heaven!

2. Teams are able to be excellent and authentic in the styles of music they play. The Black gospel team doesn't have to work to do Latino music. They can focus on doing what they do well. And they probably have a month (or more) to prepare for the next service that they will lead, so they are able to really practice and develop their strengths.

3. There is shared, diverse leadership. There is not one worship leader who chooses all the songs, structures the service, and leads every Sunday. Every culture has opportunities to lead and to follow.

Some Challenges

1. A visitor would need to attend a church for at least a month to get a real feel of the identity of the church. One Sunday is not an accurate representation of the diversity that is present in the church.

2. Music teams are segregated culturally. People who like (or are good at) one style are all grouped together. There would need to be intentional opportunities developed for them to interact with one another, as this structure makes it easy for each musician to stay with his or her cultural group.

3. There is a need for many different, genre-specific leaders with this model.

To Note

- If you are a small congregation with a lot of diversity but few musicians and worship leaders, this is not the right model for you.

- If you value cross-cultural togetherness more than stylistic integrity, this is not the model for you.

Exhibit B: 1 Main Dish (static) / Multiple Side Dishes (rotates) Model

Imagine a Sunday dinner plate filled to the brim with a beautiful salad. Vibrant greens are topped with bright red tomatoes, spicy peppers, and grilled chipotle-flavored steak. On the side is a crunchy garlic bread topped with mozzarella cheese. (I am making myself hungry with these examples!) The next Sunday, the dinner plate is filled to the brim with another beautiful salad. This time, however, vibrant greens are topped with bright mandarin oranges, sunflower seeds, and fried wonton strips. Though different from last Sunday, it is still definitely a salad. On the side is a warm bowl of chicken noodle soup.

Bridgeway Community Church (www.bridgewayonline.org), where Nikki leads worship, employs this model mostly. They will not be pigeon-holed, mind you, as they are extremely creative. But this is a generalization of their approach. In this model, the bulk of the service is in one musical style that is sort of "middle of the road" for most people. This is a constant every Sunday. Then, there are special elements in each service that are in different musical styles and languages each week as well. These different side items rotate.

Bridgeway has developed a unique musical sound and feel over the years (see chapter 11). I would describe it as kind of a gospel-informed jazz. They love color chords. Rarely will you hear a plain C Major chord, without a second, a sixth, or a major seventh. They can take almost any song and make it sound like Bridgeway. It is a beautiful thing. You should hear their arrangement of "How Great Is Our God." They have a variety of instruments (and even use some more unusual ones like the Dobro and didgeridoo from time to time as we mentioned previously), but primarily, the keyboard, bass, and drums are foundational to their sound. Jazz, as a musical style, is a fusion (or maybe better termed a "gumbo") of sorts, with strong influences from Black, Afro-Caribbean, Creole, European, and Latin cultures. So, this Bridgeway sound is a connecting point for many of the cultures in their congregation.

One Sunday, the bulk of the songs may be in English, employing this Bridgeway sound and feel, with one song in the language of Igbo being led by a Nigerian worship leader in a more typical African feel. The next Sunday, maybe a song is taught in Amharic by a Bridgeway staff member. The next week, maybe the whole congregation learns a sign in American Sign Language and signs during one song. They have opportunities to celebrate, learn from, and honor different musical styles, languages, and cultural expressions while still maintaining their Bridgeway feel.

Some Benefits
1. There is a strong sense of unifying identity with a signature sound. People in their congregation can hear certain musical expressions

and say confidently, "That is us!" When people come to visit their church, they can immediately sense a collective musical and worship identity.

2. Musicians do not have to become well versed in a large variety of musical styles but can focus on what they do well together. At the same time, because it is jazz, there is still plenty of room for diversity, creativity, and spontaneity among musicians.

3. The individual cultures and languages of the congregation are honored while the majority of the congregation doesn't necessarily have to be outside their comfort zone for a long time in each service. There is a natural cohesiveness to the worship service.

Some Challenges

1. If someone in the congregation is from a culture that doesn't have any connection to a gospel-inspired, jazz musical style, then that person is not well represented in the musical identity of the church. Leaders have to be intentional and careful not to let those members feel like a minority in the church.

2. Musicians and singers who are not connected to the unifying musical identity, could only be side items and not leaders. If your instrument is the didgeridoo or violin, you might get to play in church once or twice a year.

3. Leaders have to be trained intentionally in the Bridgeway style/feel in order to help maintain cohesiveness from week to week.

To Note

- If you do not have the creative people to arrange and write music to make it sound like your church, this is not the model for you.

- If you value frequent diverse participation more than a unifying worship identity, this is not the model for you.

Exhibit C: Smorgasbord / Constant Blending Model

Imagine a Sunday dinner plate with Korean kimbap (seaweed rolls filled with rice and veggies), a spicy fish taco, a couple of crispy, fried shrimp, and some garlic hummus with pita bread. The next Sunday, you have a spinach lasagna made with four different kinds of cheeses, a bowl of egg drop soup, fried plantain, and shieldzini (Japanese cucumber salad). Recently, I went to a multicultural event in my community, and there was food from all over the world. I couldn't contain myself. I had kimbap (Korea), taquito (Mexico), samosa (India), Jamaican jerk chicken, spring roll (China), tamale (Ecuador), fruit, and a chocolate chip cookie all on the same paper plate. You get the idea.

In this model, there is no one dominant musical style, cultural expression, or perhaps even language. You just never know what you are going to get. There is no room to be bored, because variety abounds. This is primarily the model we use in our ministry at Proskuneo (www.proskuneo.org). Because the community of Clarkston, where we are centered, is so diverse, there really is no cultural majority. We use English as a unifying language, as there are more than sixty languages spoken in a one-and-a-half mile radius. But the service may flow from a Congolese chorus with percussion and vocals into a traditional hymn sung in five different languages simultaneously, accompanied by a full rock band. There may be a time of greeting one another with typical Latino-style hugs and kisses. From there, it might switch to a Korean soloist singing in a classical style with piano and then to a bilingual (Portuguese/English) song in a bossa nova style. Everyone then stands for a scripture reading in Tamil, Mandarin, and Arabic before the sermon is given by a Black pastor. The next week is the same kind of variety, but the elements, languages, and cultural expressions may be totally different. Themes and scripture, and not style, tie the service elements together. For example, maybe you have a song medley with an Ethiopian Amharic song (lyrics: "You have seen me with Your eyes, Lord, what can I say?") linked to a Hillsongs tune (lyrics: "What can I say? What can I do? But offer this heart, oh God, completely to you") linked to a Black gospel song (lyrics: "I give myself away so You can use me").[1] The keys and tempos match, and you transition back and forth among these three songs in the medley seamlessly.

---

1. "Eyesus," Ethiopian worship song; Joel Houston, "The Stand," Hillsong Music Publishing, 2005; Sam Hinn and William McDowell, "I Give Myself Away," Delivery Room Publishing, 2008.

Some Benefits

1. No one musical style is dominant. There is a real sense of together but equal. (Note: this is in contrast to a "separate but equal" mind-set.) One way of looking at this is that there are no side dishes.

2. There is a lot of room for variety in every service. Rather than having only one or, at most, two slots for "other" expressions, every slot is a slot for "other" expressions. You could feasibly incorporate ten to fifteen different cultures and languages in one hour-long service. This is especially helpful in contexts in which there is so much diversity.

3. Musicians and congregation get a broad exposure to different languages and musical styles and have the opportunity to become competent in these. People develop flexibility and the ability to learn things more quickly.

Some Challenges

1. The service can feel schizophrenic. There is no unifying identity present in musical style or cultural expression. For people with ADD, this can be especially challenging because there is so much happening at once.

2. Leaders have to work extra hard to tie service elements together, so there is some sense of cohesiveness and continuity. Extra attention must be given to transitions and creation of song medleys for example.

3. Leaders need to have (or acquire) a high tolerance for chaos and be somewhat familiar with a large variety of languages, musical styles, and cultural expressions.

To Note

- If you don't have leaders with a high tolerance for chaos, this is not the model for you.

- If you value a shared worship identity more than equality of "stage time," this model is not for you.

Exhibit D: New Cultural Space / Fusion Model

Fusion cuisine combines the elements of different culinary traditions while not fitting specifically into any, and it is increasingly popular these days As people from different cultures marry each other or live in community together, it makes sense to combine together what they eat. Imagine opening the refrigerator and seeing an Italian pizza crust, but no tomato sauce or pepperoni! Instead you also see the ingredients for Mexican tacos. Why not put the Mexican white cheese, salsa, and refried beans on the pizza crust and create a taco pizza? The next meal might be Hawaii meets Japan meets Cuba. Marinate a Wagyu beef in soy sauce and pineapple juice. Serve it with Japanese purple potatoes and a tropical fruit salsa.

Fusion music is also increasingly popular these days. It is harder than ever to tie some of my favorite performers into specific genres. You have country artists and rap artists collaborating together and inventing new sounds. You can find groups like Aradhna (www.aradhnamusic.com) who are singing devotional songs to Jesus in a typical Indian style of music. They fuse together sitar, acoustic guitar, bass guitar, and tabla. This type of music feels authentic to bicultural people such as Chris Hale, who is one of the founders of Aradhna. He is a North American who grew up in South Asia and is fluent in Nepali and Hindi. He himself is a fusion of sorts, and the music that flows out of him naturally is a mixture of cultures.

In a worship service that takes this approach, there is no one dominant musical style, because everything is a mixture of cultures, languages, and styles. What if you found that the musicians present in your congregation were a Korean classical pianist, an African vocalist, a Cuban conga player, a rock bassist, and a Spanish guitarist? What if you put them together as a band and worked to help them live in a mutually honoring, Jesus-exalting community? What if every song at your church on a Sunday morning was led by this diverse group who have learned to both lead and follow one another? The emerging style would be like none other. If this group plays the old hymn,

180

"Nothing but the Blood," it will sound very different than the way it sounded with an organ and piano in the church where I grew up. If this group plays a Dominican praise song in a merengue-esque style, it will sound fresh and unique and will be both familiar and unfamiliar to Dominicans at the same time. When you put things together that have never been together before, you will necessarily get something new. You may have trouble describing your congregational worship to people outside your church. They may have to come and see for themselves.

Some Benefits

1. You are able to use the people-resources God has given you in a way that allows each of them to significantly inform and affect the worship style of your congregation.

2. There is a lot of room for creativity. And musicians and worshipers love creativity! Your team could really enjoy experimenting with new things and breaking new ground together.

3. There is a strong, unifying sense of your congregation's worship identity. It is unlike anything else that exists anywhere else in the world. It is uniquely and authentically representative of your diverse community.

Some Challenges

1. Because it does not come naturally for cultures to interact with one another easily, there will be a lot of work to help your musicians work and worship together in a healthy community. There will be cultural conflicts that must be navigated with the help of God's word and in the power of the Holy Spirit.

2. There is not a retention of each person's cultural identity. When they give themselves to this kind of a fusion, they are sacrificing some of who they are and must be willing to become something different.

3. When you put new things together and create things that have never existed before, sometimes things will go very well. And, other times, what is created really won't work at all. You must be

prepared for failure and offer ample room and sufficient grace for trial and error.

To Note

- If you don't have shepherding, relational leaders, this is not the model for you.

- If you strongly value retention of one's cultural identity, this is not the model for you.

Reflect

Consider carefully and prayerfully your own context. I strongly suggest dialoguing about some of these questions in community with people on your worship team, staff team, or others in your congregation who you can trust. Based on the size of your congregation, which model might be best? Based on the resources you have and the boundaries you have, which model might be best for you? Which model are you the closest to now? Are you okay with that? Based on how many cultures/languages/heart musics are present in your congregation, what model might be the best for you? Which model could your leadership team best implement?

Once you think you have a model in mind, go back and reread the first part of this chapter on the danger of models. And consider carefully what you might learn or appropriate from the other models that you did not choose.

Chapter 16
Surviving the Hard Times

Here are some practical tips for when things get rough, and they will.

One thing surprised me as I (Nikki) sat down to share my thoughts in this chapter. What surprised me was that it took me less than one second to come up with my answer to the question, "What is the hardest part about leading multicultural worship?" I guess it's something that I think about a lot as I am leading people and trying to blaze a new trail with regards to how we see ministry and how we carry out ministry to and with God's precious people. So, what's the hardest part about leading multicultural worship for me? Feeling alone.

When I was in high school, there were always these cheesy campaigns created that were aimed at keeping kids off of drugs. Do you remember any of these? I distinctly remember a commercial I saw in which some creepy guy approached a small child and offered her some substance and said something like, "Come on, everybody's doing it, it will make you feel good." Then, of course, the child successfully tells this drug dealer that she isn't interested and runs off into the sunset with a feeling of accomplishment that she "said no to drugs." When it comes to multicultural ministry, everybody's *not* doing it. This is what makes me feel alone at times.

Most days I feel great and amazing about the call that I believe Jesus has put on my life to build and lead a community of multicultural artists through the vehicle of God's church. It is one of the most amazing journeys that I have been on in my life, and leading within this context flows out of the core of my own life and my own story. Leading multicultural ministry is one of the great joys of my life. But there are some days during which the feeling of loneliness is strong. You wonder if you are on the right track. You wonder if you are just out of touch with the culture. You wonder if your philosophies about ministry are just plain wrong. You think to yourself at times that if you are doing it "right" then everybody else would be doing it too and maybe it's you that is "out there." Therefore, you ask yourself, why are you doing this? Because it seems like everybody else is pursuing something different and the ways in which they are pursuing ministry are the right ways and you are crazy for trying to do things another way. You wonder why more people are not pursuing a path that is similar to yours, and it can get lonely and frustrating. For me, the hardest part of all of this is fighting the *temptation of sameness*. To just give in and do what everybody else is doing because you perceive that what everyone else is doing is the more successful route and that it is the path of least resistance. Sometimes I wonder if I'm doing the right thing and leading people on the right trail, and if what people really want is sameness, why don't I just give that to them?

The hardest part of all of this is fighting the *temptation of sameness*.

Surviving Discouragement

I am convinced, deep within my being, that as long as I am the leader of the worship ministry at Bridgeway Community Church, I will not just press repeat and be a more diverse replica of someone else's church or of a famous worship leader somewhere or of a ministry leader in the Safari desert, or of a pastor in Asia. I am responsible to carry out the plan that God has made for me, individually. I believe this with the core of who I am. God has put vision in my spirit. What I believe about my life and my work is that it is *unique*. It is unique because there has never been anyone made exactly like me in human history, and my God has plans for me. I am responsible to carry out the plans that were created in advance for my life. I encourage my heart by remembering that God is doing something extremely special in my life and that I am responsible to be faithful to that call. As musicians, we spend so much of our time rehearsing so that we can flow and function well in a musical setting, on a stage, in front of an audience. Let's also rehearse what is true about our lives and what God has to say about who we are. When I get discouraged or even disillusioned, I have to hold onto God's word and remember why he has called me.

During these hard times, I rehearse the truth that it can be hard. Just allowing myself the permission to embrace that is freeing at times. The reality is, when you choose to be out in front of the crowd or out in front of a group of people you are leading, it can feel lonely and scary. But it is what it is. That may sound simplistic to you, but it's the truth. When you feel all sorts of emotions like these, accept them, bear the burden with another person you trust, and continue to move forward as you are led by the Holy Spirit.

If you are a leader, you are a trailblazer. Those of us engaging in multicultural ministry are still trailblazers after all this time. We are in essence cutting through the underbrush that is before us with a machete. We are carving out a path that does not already exist. Many of the principles that currently exist with regard to ministry and church growth for monocultural ministries may not apply within our contexts. How to minister to diverse people groups, how to engage as a worship leader, how to honor culture—these are unique challenges we face. There are not many books to read about such things. We are doing ministry by trial, error, and experience. This is the truth that I hold on to when I get discouraged and question what I am doing. I refuse to believe that my journey as a leader is supposed to look just like someone else's journey. Yes, there may be similarities, but God is doing something new in me and through me, and I believe if I am faithful to how he leads me, these things can only be done through someone like me.

> # Many of the principles that currently exist with regard to ministry and church growth for monocultural ministries may not apply within our contexts.

More times than not I struggle with the question, "Am I just out there?" And the answer may be a resounding *yes*. But maybe that is how people like me and like you blaze trails. We are crazy enough to step out and create something new. One thing that I know is that leading multicultural ministry is what makes me feel alive. To try new things, to attempt different expressions of worship and music, and to create new ways to minister to people make me feel like I am accomplishing the good things that God has planned in advance for me to do. Doubt will come, but I believe that I always have a choice in how I respond. I want to be a trailblazer who clears away the hindrances for multicultural communities and sets new trends of ministry to and with diverse communities of people. How about you?

Here are some practical things you can do to help yourself survive the hard times:

1. *Consider the reality that God is using the difficulties to form good things in you.*

For me, the beauty that has come out of these times of questioning and confusion is courage. Over the course of my life I have dealt with a lot of fear. The way I've been able to move forward is by making attempts at reprogramming this pattern of being afraid. Instead of running from the things that cause me fear, I attempt to lean into them and pray that Jesus will replace my fear with hope, peace, and faith. Given my environment at my church, blazing a trail has made me more courageous about how to do ministry and how to live my life. There are other areas of my life, not just ministry related, that have benefited as a result of God calling me as a multicultural worship leader. I have found courage to take chances, courage to allow my own life choices to look different than other leaders around me, courage just to discover who I am as a child of God and to let God mold me into the unique person that he has created me to be. I love what the Lord said to Joshua as he was about to blaze a new trail: "I've commanded you to be brave and strong, haven't I? Don't be alarmed or terrified, because the Lord your God is with you wherever you go" (Josh 1:9).

2. *Recognize and celebrate successes.*

This is what keeps me going and encouraged as a trailblazer. When I see people having their culture honored, my heart rejoices. When I see people of various ethnicities doing life together and marrying each other, I celebrate. When I see people in my ministry preferring others as better than themselves (Phil 2:3) and showing up with a desire to learn and love, I point it out and thank God for it. Things like these are the fruit of multicultural ministry. It is scary to step out on a limb as a leader, but it is empowering when you find that there is fresh, beautiful fruit being produced on that limb! Take time to get outside your own feelings and see what God is doing. Encourage yourself with these successes. Share these success stories with others. Tell them. Retell them. Celebrate well! You might even want to throw a party. Or several!

3. *Laugh at yourself.*

Recently, I (Josh) was preaching in South Korea. In the middle of my sermon, I asked for feedback from the congregation. I invited them to share their opinions and thoughts in front of everyone. I know better. I have studied about power distance in Asian cultures. I know that Koreans do not usually like to single themselves out from the group. What was I thinking? I had to laugh when, after a long, awkward silence, the only person (out of the more than 250 present) who answered my question was the only other American in the room. Even after all these years of studying and teaching about crossing cultures, I still make mistakes. I am learning to give myself grace and to laugh at myself.

If you and I (Nikki) ever get a chance to share a platform leading worship together, one of the things that you will discover about me is that I love to be "in the moment" during worship. I love to acknowledge what I see happening around me during worship and point out cool, cultural things that are happening as a way of honoring people and culture in the main gathering. One morning during our 10:00 a.m. service, we were singing a powerful phrase about God's love and his character in one of our favorite worship songs as a church. I looked to my left and saw our ASL interpreter signing the phrase that we were singing. I paused in the song and asked her to show that to the congregation again. Then, in this brilliant moment of spontaneity, I looked over at my electric guitar player who is from Guatemala and asked him if he could tell us what that phrase would be in Spanish. He said it, and everyone clapped and rejoiced in the room. Then, I turned around to look at my acoustic guitar player who is of Korean descent. He is a little shy, and he knew I was coming after him in that moment. He was laughing and shaking his head as to say "Don't you come over here!" but I was convinced that he'd be fine and he was just shy. I asked him in that moment in front of eleven hundred people how the phrase we were singing would sound in Korean. I tilted the microphone toward his mouth, and he said, "I don't speak Korean."

The whole room erupted in laughter, and I felt like an embarrassed fool. Not embarrassed for my own sake, but because I feared I had potentially shamed him in public, which is a cultural no-no. Thankfully, we all laughed together in that moment, and my guitar player thought it was funny. Whew!

4. *Go back to God's word.*

When you are feeling particularly discouraged, remind yourself that this multicultural worship thing was not your idea in the first place. It is firmly rooted in the heart of God and has been revealed to us in his word. Take time to rehearse the scriptural realities that we shared in chapter 2. In fact, you might want to go back and reread that chapter when you are struggling to keep going in multicultural ministry. It is not your responsibility to create unity. You are to preserve the unity that we have already been given in Jesus. There's a big difference!

5. *Spend time with other people who "get it."*

It can be exhausting to always be casting vision and explaining why you are doing what you do. Believe me, I (Josh) know. My own loved ones have said discouraging things about my ministry over the years. Some of my extended family like the music and the CDs and the concerts, but they have told me that they just don't see the point of nations coming together in worship. That can be deflating. But I have found much encouragement from other like-minded trailblazers. Nikki and I are part of a core team that leads Multicultural Worship Leaders Network (www.multiculturalworship.org), and the times we spend together worshipping, praying, sharing, and having fun together help me persevere. In addition, I have a multicultural worship leader friend who I pray with on the phone every Sunday morning. We have been meeting together for many years now, and that relationship is a huge encouragement to my heart.

Just Keep Moving

As you embrace these concepts as a leader of multicultural ministries, ask God to give you the right perspective within each season that you find yourself. Remember that nothing surprises our Heavenly Father. Remember that he has called you to a high and worthy calling to lead the nations in worship. Remember that you are not alone, that there are people all over the world who are pursuing the same vision, and you can reach out. Remember that the Lord, who is our Good Shepherd, will lead us *through* the valley to the place where he desires us to be. Remember that his way can be trusted, and just keep moving. Be strong. Be courageous. He is with you wherever you go.

Remember that you are not alone, that there are people all over the world who are pursuing the same vision.

Reflect

Are you currently experiencing burnout? If so, why? If not, what steps can you take to prevent burnout from happening? What habits and safeguards can you build into your life and schedule?

Chapter 17

Stories of Encouragement

We are each surrounded by such a great cloud of witnesses. Multicultural worship is happening successfully all around this globe. Take a look!

You are not alone. The community of multicultural worship leaders is growing but is still very small. Therefore, it can be challenging to find other leaders who are pursuing this vision. It can also be hard to remember that multicultural worship is happening all around the world. But Romans 12 reminds us that we are surrounded by a great cloud of witnesses. There are many who are cheering you on. Here are some encouraging stories from people, like you and like us, who are pursuing multicultural worship ministry. May you be encouraged that it *can* work and it *is working* to bring God glory worldwide.

From Conflict to Friendship
Peter Park, Korean American Worship Leader, Minnesota

During the fall of 2010, I had the opportunity to serve at a Presbyterian church in Minneapolis. It was my first church staff position, which I was very excited about. I waited nearly ten years for an opportunity like this, but I didn't realize how hard it would be emotionally.

One of the challenges I initially experienced was with an African American mother and her two children who were all involved with the worship team. I could tell when I started that they were carrying a lot of pain. The fact that we were emphasizing African American gospel music for Black History Month did not help.

At the time, we only had six people represented from the African American community of believers, and three of them were already on the worship team, so the church ended up inviting singers from another nearby church. To be honest, it felt like it was more about having a good worship performance than about building relationships.

One of the things I had decided for our worship team was that it was not in our best interest to do any solos at the time, until we had a better sense as a worship "team" and what our responsibilities were as servants. This didn't go over so well with the mother, who thought I wasn't acknowledging where her son was in his spiritual walk and wasn't allowing him to use his talents during worship service. I remember we were outside the church building standing next to my car in the cold Minnesota winter.

I offered her a ride earlier that evening, but she was ready to walk away. I called her back and told her to, "Get in the car." This was one of those distinct moments in which our relationship changed, for the good. It didn't matter that we disagreed on a subject matter; what mattered was being intentional about building our friendship because of it and then in spite of it.

In the weeks that followed, I met with the family either before or after practice to pray together and talk through any issues that they were experiencing. This included any questions they had about why I was doing things a certain way.

What really worked in our favor was that this mother, who is now my friend, has great respect for those in authority over her. I'm also grateful that God allowed me to persevere through this initially uncomfortable relationship to come out on the other side with a fruitful one.

Our families spent a lot of time together during the two years I served at that particular Presbyterian church. I'm so grateful God was able to humble us, allowing us to grow and mature spiritually so we could understand what unity and perseverance are all about.

What Language Was That?
by Frank Fortunato, Jordan

It was the early days of the Operation Mobilization ship ministry. It was the late 1970s. Back then few groups were thinking multiculturally about worship. With a crew and staff from thirty nations and from every continent, the MV Logos ship music teams made some brave efforts to sing in other languages.

After docking in one of the Jordanian ports, a team of ship people went to the capital of Amman to minister at one of the Christian churches. We had practiced our Arabic worship choruses for several weeks, blending our accents from Asia, Europe, and North and South America. We had a delightful time singing in English and other languages and highlighted our Arabic song at the Sunday service.

After the meeting, an elderly lady came up to me and said: "You sang one of our favorite tunes tonight. We love that melody. Now what language were you using with our Arabic tune?" Such was our early effort to honor various cultures by trying to learn one of their own worship songs. It was from that effort that we learned to use a national soloist, when possible and to use songs with a short text load.

Even When Rejected
by Jelani Greenidge, African American Worship Leader, Oregon

So sometimes even in our disappointments, God uses us for his glory.

I'd spent about six years as worship director for a multicultural church in Portland, but after resigning, I was looking for work. A pastor in my area reached out to me after he saw one of my YouTube videos and inquired about my interest in the opening at his church for a worship leader.

I was surprised to hear from him because, as an African American worship leader with a reputation for stylistic versatility, I didn't think they would be all that interested in what I had to offer. From the outside, my perception was that it was a suburban, almost exclusively White church. I figured he knew something that I didn't—were they experiencing a surge of people of color in the area? I was curious enough to find out.

One phone call and a few e-mails later, I was genuinely interested. According to this pastor, his church, though successful, was beginning to coast a bit. They were a stable, family-oriented church, and he'd helped them take small steps toward being a more kingdom-focused, inclusive congregation. He felt that my leadership in worship would be a great catalyst to move the congregation further out of their comfort zone and into a more others-oriented outlook.

So I followed the application process, which put me in contact with the chair of the hiring committee. And after speaking to him, it was clear that he was not interested in me as a candidate. It wasn't that they were further in the process with another candidate, either. He just flat-out didn't think I was a good fit and was pretty sure the rest of the committee would agree. They had a clear idea of who they wanted: a White, late-twenty-something, guitar-playing rock vocalist who could be counted on to crank out plenty of Chris Tomlin and Matt Redman, and that wasn't me.

Once I got off the phone with the committee chair, I was irritated and hurt. But I gave it a few days, and my perspective softened. I realized that my initial instincts were right, but I also knew that the pastor's heart was in the right place. What I had seen was a clear disconnect between what the pastor had been saying and the attitudes of others in leadership.

A week or so later, I had a follow-up conversation with the pastor. By this point, I'd long since made peace about not moving further in the hiring process, mostly because I knew that if I'd somehow gotten the job anyway, I would've felt constricted and unappreciated. But in this follow-up, I took off my "candidate" hat and put on my "outside observer" hat. I told the pastor about the conversation I'd had and about the disconnect I saw.

In his response, he was humbled but also grateful. He was glad to get the honest feedback and motivated to do more of the work toward getting his people on the same page. And I was grateful to be able to give a timely word of warning to a pastor who was ready to receive it. I hung up the phone feeling completely at peace about the whole thing.

I ended up serving as a worship pastor at a different suburban church that gratefully received my diverse style of worship leadership; but the kicker was, the relational connection that led to this opportunity was someone I met while visiting the first church. God used the church that rejected me to bring me toward my most fruitful season of ministry.

In Spite of the Rain
by Josh Davis, White American, Dominican Republic

A few years ago, I was leading worship in the Dominican Republic. We had planned an outdoor worship service bringing Haitians and Dominicans together in bilingual worship. Haitians and Dominicans have a long history of animosity toward one another, and this was a groundbreaking opportunity! But, did I mention it was outside? Right. So, two hours before the service was supposed to start, we began to set up the sound and video equipment under an overhang, and, with some creative wiring, we got everything in working order. Thirty minutes before the service was to start, people began to show up, and we were thrilled. Ten minutes before start time, it began to drizzle. The people were sitting out in the open, getting wet.

We decided to have everyone crowd underneath the overhang to wait things out. We enjoyed talking to the people next to us (the overhang was only big enough to cover us if we stood shoulder-to-shoulder). After about thirty minutes or so, the drizzle stopped. And something else happened. The power went out. Things were not going our way, or so we thought. We could have just shut things down and sent people home. But some people had traveled for hours to come to this service. We made the choice to look around for what we did have, instead of focusing on what we didn't have. We found a little hut with a thatched roof. It was big enough for all of us to just barely squeeze under. And it was small enough for everyone to hear the singing, playing, and speaking without any amplification. So, we squeezed under this little pavilion. And we began to worship, in the pitch-black darkness. Every once in a while, someone would take a picture or open up their cell phone, and there would be a little flash of light. But, for most of the night, it was just close fellowship (literally shoulder-to-shoulder and knee-to-knee) and lifting our voices in praise to God together. All of us who were there look back on that time of worship as a very special time. We wouldn't have changed a thing. And the end result was better than we could have ever planned.

It's All about Love
by Jo-Ann Richards, Jamaica

Although I was born and raised in Jamaica, most of my worship-music experience falls within the categories of traditional hymns and contemporary Christian music. For the most part, that was my "heart music" when it came to corporate worship.

In 2001, I read an article that was published in *Mission Frontiers* magazine, written by Wycliffe Bible Translators' missionary Jack Popjes ("Music to Their Ears: An Ethnomusicologist Helps The Canelas of Brazil Worship More Meaningfully," *Mission Frontier*, July–August 1996.). Jack and his wife, Jo, were engaged in translating the Scriptures for the Canela people in Brazil. They were musicians before going to Brazil. However, among the Canela, they felt like musical "klutzes." They eventually invited ethnomusicologist Tom Avery to study the Canela music and write new songs in their language and music styles. The following year, Tom returned with a set of new songs that he had composed, which he introduced to the Canela people. According to Jack, it was like pouring gas on a campfire.

When I read the article, I thought, "I want to do that!" By 2002, I was enrolled in a master's program in ethnomusicology and was in Burkina Faso serving as an ethnomusicologist in training. It was a whole new world.

In 2003, I attended the very first Global Consultation on Music in Mission (GCoMM), an international gathering of persons who encourage and equip Christ-followers to use their own language and artistic expressions to worship Jesus Christ. I had been in international gatherings before, and thanks to the Western nature of the music with which I was comfortable, I usually had no problem singing along with the other worshippers, because I knew all the songs. GCoMM 2003 was different. In addition to the familiar songs, we also had songs in a wide range of languages, and "strange" and "weird" music styles from all over the world. To say I was annoyed would be putting it mildly. My argument was that it was fine to have these strange songs in a workshop or seminar setting. However, for corporate worship, we need to use songs that everyone can understand and relate to. How could I be expected to worship in a verbal or musical language that I couldn't understand?

GCoMM 2006 rolled around, and I was back. I wish I could explain how God did it, but somehow, in those three intermediary years, he brought about a deeper level of understanding. The songs were even "stranger" and "weirder" than the time before. This time, however, I suddenly understood that the persons to whom this language and music were special were my own sisters and brothers, a part of my global kingdom family. In fact, some of them were in the very room with us, singing with us! Suddenly, it was like a veil was removed from my eyes, and I experienced an epiphany. It was all about love. If I truly loved my brothers and sisters, I would happily sing their songs with them in praise of our awesome God.

An African Experience
by Evan Rogers, South Africa

I was born a White, English-speaking "African" in a very broken South Africa.

Racial segregation and discrimination were legalized and enforced by the White government. The infamous "group areas act," saw non-Whites (so-called) removed from desired areas and placed elsewhere. Separate education systems were introduced to control the masses. In my school we had one Black person, Morris, an ambassador's son. Apart from domestic workers and gardeners, we would have very little contact with the indigenous people of South Africa. They did not live in our suburbs but mostly in designated townships. You learn to accept the absurdity as normal, and only as I grew up into my teens did serious questions arise. Why were there "Whites only" beaches and public ablutions, for example?

My teenage years were at the height of the "struggle," with sanctions, uprisings, and violence. It was time to change, and questions had to be answered by actions!

Most White communities had little interest in building bridges with non-Whites who by and large were "the poor."

I was fortunate to have been part of a church that saw differently. We started out as a church in the suburbs of Cape Town, with maybe one or two non-White families willing to associate and help us transform. It was way past time for the church to rise and take action. The church leaders set a vision of being a multicultural, nonracial church, reflecting the manifold diverse wisdom of God.

We realized that praise could be a key part of demonstrating the vision, so we headed down the road of singing songs in African languages. We started with simple, easy songs, often only containing a phrase or two but with a particularly African feel. A number of people left the church at this time because they could not grasp why a majority White/English church would be trying to sing "Xhosa" and "Zulu" songs. They felt they could not worship or engage with God in this way. It was often perceived as tokenism and seemed unrealistic to some. When you are trying to prophetically move forward, it will sometimes feel unnatural. We were working against an unnatural, ungodly system called apartheid (an Afrikaans word: "the state of being apart"; "apart-hood").

We could have given up and reverted to Western songs only, but the vision was cast and we were going to stick to it. It took some convincing and training of leaders and musicians to grow an appetite for the style and for the ability to connect with songs in other languages. We set a goal of a minimum of two African-language songs for the worship leaders struggling to adapt. Gradually we saw the demographics of the congregation changing.

The greatest change came when we as a church started to build relationships with township communities. I had the privilege of joining one of our evangelists on visits to the outlying townships and learned a number of "township tunes" while meeting and praying with the communities. This influenced my approach to praise as I witnessed a communal way of worship, incorporating "their" songs, dances, and passion! Eventually we started bussing township folks to our church meeting. No longer were we *trying* to be multicultural; we were multicultural. Relationships were being formed, worshippers were being transformed, and sermons were being translated.

Our community praise, for many, demonstrates acceptance, love, and willingness to bridge gaps. It has become a way of life, and now our congregation challenges us when we don't sing in other languages. There is no turning back. This is a taste of heaven on earth.

Rhythms of the Heart
by William Johnson Garcia, North Carolina

I was helping facilitate a percussion clinic in a music store with an established local drummer who is quite accomplished and has toured internationally in the past. It was not a traditional Christian workshop necessarily; however, I often mention worship and worship genres as a practical demonstration even in secular arenas. Often people in the audience may play at a church, and even if they do not, it is a good bridge for later conversations about my faith to nonbelievers.

My portion of the clinic was primarily on congas and bongos. I used a lot of traditional Latin technique in my presentation, as I often do. A couple months after the clinic a woman who was an attendee called me and asked if I would do a presentation for her class at the university she was attending. She was in a humanities class, and for an assignment her group was giving a presentation on Puerto Rico. I would be demonstrating a few traditional Puerto Rican rhythms on a couple conga drums. I accepted the invitation, and after my presentation, she approached me and shared with me how when she first heard me playing at the clinic in the music store she was reminded of her youth in Puerto Rico. While she was speaking, I could tell that this was not mere nostalgia for her, but a deep emotional connection that caused her to pause as she spoke because it seemed she was nearly in tears. It was something about the way that I played and I suppose also the way I carried myself that spoke to her heart.

Through the congas I spoke her heart language. This was not necessarily the first time I had heard something like this; however, it was the first time someone had been so moved in a "cultural sense" by my playing. Through my respect and admiration of a tradition I was able to touch her heart. I did not fully understand it then, nor do I attempt to say that I get it now; however, it was the first time that a light shined so bright in my own mind that it helped me understand how I was drawn to these instruments in the first place. My grandfather was from Puerto Rico, and by playing Latin percussion, I feel a connection to those roots that is beyond words. It is this passion that actually led me to the most Sacred Root that is Jesus Christ. It is this continued passion for a beautiful culture—or I should say *cultures*—that allows me, in my humble opinion, to speak with integrity through the instrument. Looking into that woman's tearful eyes taught me how dear the skills we can acquire through God's calling can be to another's heart. It allowed me to actually share a little bit about my faith and my church with her husband that day during the presentation. To this day stories like this one encourage me on the long nights when I am in my basement working on a rhythmic pattern, sharpening my "chops," or working on a new composition. You just never know who is watching and listening.

Trying New Things
by Minister Noel Park, originally from Korea, now living in Maryland

When I thought about "multiculture," I used to imagine "multi-ethnic" first. Different colors and different faces had represented a multiculture for me. While I was in a multicultural ministry in the past three years, I clearly realized that a range of multiple cultures is wider than multiple ethnicities. Multicultural is not only an attitude to analyze differences, but also an action to endeavor to embrace differences. Therefore, I can say a precondition for being multicultural is love.

I, as a Korean who couldn't speak English well, came to the United States when I was thirty years old. The age of thirty can be regarded to be young, but it was not easy at that age to learn a new language and to be adapted to very new culture. My first ministry was worship team. The ministry leader invited me first and asked me so kindly to tell my story. After she listened to it, suddenly she suggested that I read Bible verses in Korean in front of more than one thousand people in Sunday service. It was a challenge for me but not a big one, because I could speak in Korean. Next time, she suggested I sing in English in a mass choir. That was also a challenge but not a big one, because I was in the choir so nobody could listen to my voice separately even if I couldn't sing well in English. But the next time, her suggestions got bigger and bigger. She suggested that I play drums, sing in both Korean and English, and play the Djembe (African drum), which I've never played before. And in these days, the challenges coming from her are ongoing.

Looking back, I completed and succeeded at all of those tasks above and never said "No, I can't." Surely, I was not a person who used to do those things, and I was also very shy. But she, as my leader, had a warm heart for a newcomer like me and wanted to maximize my potential, and I trusted her, which couldn't be done without love. Whenever she gave me a challenge, she always introduced me to people who could help me, and they helped me develop even more what I did well. That was the reason why my challenge was getting bigger. Now nearly three years later, I have become a person who helps others in a multicultural ministry just like what she did when I came here.

In Life and in Church

by Pastor Clark Robinson, Caucasian Worship Pastor, Maryland

Statistics say that there are over sixty-five hundred spoken languages in the world, and I would imagine that there are just as many hues of skin color and cultural expressions of life to go along with those languages. How presumptuous would it be, then, for us to believe that the language that we speak, the culture that we grew up in, or the color of our skin should dictate the expression of worship to the God of the universe who created all this diversity? If we truly understand that our experience for all eternity will be every nation, tribe, people, and language worshipping before the Lamb (Rev 7:9), and that this life is just preparation for that eternity, how can we not long for that to be our reality now?

Having grown up in the Washington, DC, area, having had friends across racial and cultural lines all of my life, and having served as a missionary in Brazil, I cannot imagine anything else in church or in my expression of worship other than something that is truly multicultural. My wife is from Brazil, we often speak Portuguese at home, and my four children go to school with and have always had friends from various ethnicities and nationalities and who speak different languages. So if our daily lives are lived out multiculturally, then why would I want anything else for my family except the richness of worship in a multicultural setting?

Streams of Hope is a multicultural, multi-ethnic church just outside of Washington, DC. I have had the privilege of being the worship pastor here for the past fourteen years, and we have more than twenty-five nationalities represented in our congregation of between 150 and 200 people. Over the past twenty-five years, our church has also been home to Korean, Vietnamese, Hispanic, Messianic Jewish, and multiple Brazilian congregations. Worshipping, fellowshipping, and interacting with those from all these different cultures and languages has given me and those in our congregation the ability to see and experience a little bit of heaven on this side of eternity. I cannot imagine a life without the diversity and the breadth and depth of experience that all my brothers and sisters bring from their cultures. I believe that we are robbing ourselves of the fullness of life that could be ours as children of God and followers of Jesus when we don't seek to be in a place that celebrates the diversity that we have as God's people.

Maybe I Could Worship Jesus, Too

by Josh Davis, White American, Georgia

"That's when my friend realized that maybe she could worship Jesus, too, even as a Chinese person."

There are rare and precious moments in your life in which you catch a glimpse of some of the unseen things that God is doing through you. Recently, I was leading worship at a local Christian school's international student banquet, and afterward, a Chinese girl pulled me aside. She told me the story of her friend, who came from China to Providence Christian School here in Georgia. She came, oblivious to Jesus. Once here, she heard worship songs in chapel week after week. She assumed that all worship songs were in English and that Jesus was to be known and worshipped by Americans only.

Then, during one chapel, I worked with the school's worship team to lead "How Great Is Our God" in a variety of languages, including Chinese. This was something simple, not too difficult or time consuming, and to be honest (because of the way the Lord has led and taught me), it was sort of a no-brainer. But for this Chinese girl, the moment was profound. It was there, in that moment, that she realized for the first time that maybe she could worship Jesus, too, even though she is Chinese. And it was that moment that started her on the path toward knowing Jesus and accepting him as her Lord and Savior. I listened, with tears in my eyes, as this girl's friend told me this story. And I was reminded deep down inside why we do what we do.

Share Your Story

All of our stories are so very different, but the awesome truth is that we all have one. Our stories are a powerful way to encourage one another in this effort of seeing God's kingdom on earth look like it is in heaven. The more stories we tell about our journeys in multicultural worship, the more understanding we can all have about what God is doing around the world to bring nations together in worship. You have a story, too. We need to hear it and be changed by it. Share your story of encouragement with us and the larger community at www.multiculturalworship.org, and let's encourage one another toward heaven on earth!

CPSIA information can be obtained at www.ICGtesting.com
Printed in the USA
LVOW04s1523060315

429288LV00002B/2/P